United Nations Office for
Disarmament Affairs

UNODA Occasional Papers

No. 28, October 2016

Rethinking General and Complete Disarmament in the Twenty-First Century

United Nations

The United Nations Office for Disarmament Affairs (UNODA) Occasional Papers are a series of ad hoc publications featuring, in edited form, papers or statements made at meetings, symposiums, seminars, workshops or lectures that deal with topical issues in the field of arms limitation, disarmament and international security. They are intended primarily for those concerned with these matters in Government, civil society and in the academic community.

The views expressed in this publication are those of the authors and do not necessarily reflect those of the United Nations or its Member States.

Material in UNODA Occasional Papers may be reprinted without permission, provided the credit line reads "Reprinted from UNODA Occasional Papers" and specifies the number of the Occasional Paper concerned. Notification to the following e-mail address would be highly appreciated: unoda-web@un.org.

Symbols of United Nations documents are composed of capital letters combined with figures. These documents are available in the official languages of the United Nations at http://ods.un.org. Specific disarmament-related documents can also be accessed through the disarmament reference collection at https://www.un.org/disarmament/publications/library/.

This publication is available from

www.un.org/disarmament

UNITED NATIONS PUBLICATION
Sales No. E.16.IX.8

ISBN 978-92-1-142314-3
eISBN 978-92-1-058455-5

Contents

Part 3
The way forward

Foreword

In his first report on the work of the Organization, in 2007 the Secretary-General referred to general and complete disarmament as "the ultimate strategic goal of the United Nations".

In the early decades of the United Nations, general and complete disarmament—the simultaneous pursuit of conventional arms control together with the elimination of weapons of mass destruction—was considered to be the best pathway for disarmament.

The United Nations conducted and facilitated serious negotiations towards these ends for many years. These efforts culminated in landmark achievements. In 1959, in the first resolution co-sponsored by the entire membership of the Organization, the General Assembly proclaimed by acclamation that general and complete disarmament was the most important objective facing the world. In 1961, the Soviet Union and the United States reached agreement on agreed principles for a comprehensive international treaty and led international negotiations in Geneva towards this goal for the next four years.

In 1978, the General Assembly declared general and complete disarmament to be the ultimate objective of the United Nations in the field of disarmament. Since then, Member States have pursued systematic and progressive steps leading to disarmament. This approach has resulted in important instruments, including the establishment of nuclear-weapon-free zones and bans on nuclear testing, various inhumane weapons, anti-personnel landmines and cluster munitions.

But our efforts so far, while impressive, have been insufficient to halt unrestrained growth in military budgets, to prevent the development of advanced new types of weapons from spiralling into new conflicts or to end the devastating toll to civilians caused by conventional warfare fuelled by the overaccumulation and widespread availability of arms. There is renewed concern that these developments and the complicated nexus between emerging and established technologies are outpacing our ability to ensure effective control and to maintain stability.

To many, general and complete disarmament sounds like an anachronism from the early days of the cold war. Yet, it is increasingly evident that our common aspirations for peace, vital humanitarian imperatives, human rights and sustainable development require us to find new ways to transform that vision into a new paradigm for sustainable security through the general demilitarization of international affairs.

I wish to express my gratitude to this volume's contributors, who include some of the world's leading scholars, diplomats and activists on the topic of general and complete disarmament. Special appreciation is owed to the research of the Centre for International Studies and Diplomacy at the School of Oriental and African Studies (SOAS), University of London, and to its Director, Dr. Dan Plesch, for rekindling international attention to this issue.

The articles featured in this publication were originally presented at the seminar "Comprehensive Approaches for Disarmament in the Twenty-first Century: Rethinking General and Complete Disarmament", organized by the Centre for International Studies and Diplomacy at SOAS, sponsored by the Permanent Mission of Costa Rica and held at the United Nations Headquarters in New York on 21 October 2015. I hope these articles lead to renewed attention and proposals to modernize the disarmament agenda.

Kim Won-soo
Under-Secretary-General
High Representative for Disarmament Affairs
September 2016

Preface

Setting the doomsday clock back from midnight with general and complete disarmament

Kennette Benedict
Lecturer, University of Chicago
Executive Director and Publisher (retired),
Bulletin of the Atomic Scientists

The Doomsday Clock first appeared on the cover of the *Bulletin of the Atomic Scientists* in June 1947 to warn the public about the dangers of atomic weapons and the potential catastrophe of future wars. The *Bulletin* editors called for international control of nuclear materials and technologies and, since then, authors have written about the connections between nuclear weapons and the need for general and complete disarmament to protect humanity from the ravages of war.

Bulletin experts reasoned that, as the public would come to know the terrible consequences of using the most destructive weapons yet invented, no leader would even dare to start a war with conventional weapons because the conflict would escalate inevitably to a nuclear war too awful to contemplate. In light of this logic, scientists and political leaders supported the United Nations' founding declarations calling for general and complete disarmament to avoid future nuclear warfare.

However, even as countries signed onto the United Nations Charter of 1946 and the United States and the Soviet Union each called for general disarmament, policy leaders felt that growing hostilities between the two emerging superpowers would prevent any agreement on complete disarmament and military strategists sought rationales that would bring stability to the arms race—that is, to control nuclear weapons rather than to eliminate them.

With the end of the cold war between the East and West, however, the rationale for nuclear arms control, rather than disarmament, lacks the force it might have had at the height of the East-West hostilities in the 1960s and 1970s. In fact, since 1992, the United States and the Russian Federation have reduced their nuclear arsenals significantly—from some 70,000 to about 16,000. In addition, with the Intermediate-Range Nuclear Forces (INF) Treaty of 1991, a whole class of conventional bomb delivery missile systems has been eliminated. In fact, past arms control negotiations between the United States and the Soviet Union/Russian Federation have often addressed conventional weapons capability. For example, verification of the Anti-Ballistic Missile Treaty, the INF Treaty and other bilateral strategic arms control agreements has been based on counting delivery vehicles rather than nuclear warheads; links between conventional and nuclear systems are nothing new in the nuclear age.

Also as a result of the cold war's end and the emerging humanitarian impact movement, more countries are calling for enforcement of the provisions of the Treaty on the Non-Proliferation of Nuclear Weapons for general and complete disarmament, especially as conditions now seem to warrant such actions. Nearly all countries have eschewed nuclear weapons and, in exchange, expect that the nuclear-weapon countries will disarm. Arms control is no longer enough; it is finally being recognized for what it always was—as a way of establishing floors for the number of nuclear weapons each country may retain, rather than a ceiling that will continually be lowered. It is well past time then for the United Nations to act upon its founding declarations pledging general and complete disarmament.

That is why this volume of essays is so significant and welcome at this time. The authors examine historic, strategic, humanitarian and economic aspects of general and complete disarmament to elaborate and elevate the case for prohibiting conventional weapons systems as well as nuclear weapons.

While the use of even one nuclear bomb would kill and maim the vast majority of people in a region and render a city uninhabitable, the current use of powerful conventional weapons in war is killing hundreds of thousands, destroying cities, collapsing societies in the Middle East, Africa and Asia, and spurring mass migrations that are causing suffering and disruption in nearly all countries of the world. While nuclear weapons still demand the world's attention, the humanitarian motivation for general disarmament is plain.

Finally, as States lower their nuclear arsenals to tens and hundreds, rather than thousands of weapons, it is becoming even more apparent that many countries also have very large conventional forces that can threaten international peace and stability. In the face of anti-ballistic missile systems, stealthy bombers, large fleets of missile-armed submarines, armed drones and special operations equipment, without general and complete disarmament, nuclear disarmament by itself might make the world free, once again, for the horrors of large-scale conventional warfare—a prospect that must be prevented through general and complete disarmament.

The Doomsday Clock is an indicator of how close we are to catastrophe from technologies of our own invention. Nuclear weapons can cause nearly apocalyptic damage in a very short time. But today, conventional weapons systems are destroying cities and towns in major regions of the world, undermining economies and rending the fabric of societies in a kind of slow motion catastrophe. Without all-out efforts to eliminate nuclear weapons and to bring an end to the use of powerful conventional weapons to deal with conflicts of interest—that is, without general and complete disarmament—we are doomed to live with increasing instability, human suffering and even the end of civilization as we know it. The Clock is ticking.

Acknowledgements

The United Nations Office for Disarmament Affairs and the Centre for International Studies and Diplomacy at the School of Oriental and African Studies, University of London, express their sincere gratitude to the individuals who contributed to this volume: Alyson Bailes, Kennette Benedict, Matthew Bolton, John Burroughs, Jacqueline Cabasso, Maritza Chan, Marc Finaud, Richard Jolly, Andrew Lichterman, Paul Meyer and Randy Rydell. They also express gratitude to Kevin Miletic and Michael Spies for their work in coordinating and editing this volume, as well as to Chris King for his support. Appreciation is also owed to Maisy Bailey and Marta Corti for their research assistance.

The editor wishes to acknowledge with gratitude the distinctive contribution by Ms. Alyson J. K. Bailes, who wrote the chapter "General and complete disarmament and defence policies". Ms. Bailes, who was a British diplomat, political scientist and academic, passed away on 29 April 2016.

Part 1
Historical and contextual overview

Time for a discursive rehabilitation: A brief history of general and complete disarmament

Matthew Bolton
Assistant Professor, Pace University

The roots of an idea

The concept of general and complete disarmament (GCD) has its roots in long-standing concerns about the destabilizing and costly nature of maintaining standing offensive armies and armaments. The fourth century B.C.E. Chinese philosophical text attributed to Mozi condemned offensive war for the diversion of productive resources into weapons that "break and rot and never come back" (Mozi 5:18:2). Similarly, in words now inscribed on a wall facing the United Nations Headquarters in New York, the Hebrew prophet Isaiah envisioned a world in which people would "beat their swords into plowshares, and their spears into pruning hooks" (Isa 4:2)—converting the economy of militarism to one of peace. These classical sources have served as an inspiration for disarmament and arms control proposals in the modern era, as the growing destructiveness of technological weapons became increasingly clear. Drawing on Immanuel Kant's call in *Perpetual Peace* for standing armies to be abolished, United States President Woodrow Wilson included sweeping reductions in national arsenals "to the lowest point consistent with domestic safety" in his 14-point peace plan at the end of the First World War. An adapted version of Wilson's language was included in the Covenant of the League of Nations of 1919, calling for the "reduction of national armaments to the lowest point consistent with national safety and the enforcement by common action of international obligations" (article 8).

These commitments, to our contemporary ears, have an unfashionably quixotic and utopian ring. However, in the inter-war years (and for the following two decades) many people took them seriously. A vibrant global civil society movement, shocked at the devastation of the First World War, pressured political leaders to seek global peace and disarmament. Several organizations founded in this period continue to play a major role in disarmament and arms control campaigns today, such as the Women's International League for Peace and Freedom. Throughout the 1920s and early 1930s, international diplomatic efforts aimed to enshrine these public hopes into the emerging architecture of global governance. The most well-known of these is the 1928 Kellogg-Briand Pact, which banned offensive warfare, often mischaracterized as a pipe dream, given the horrors of the Second World War that followed. But the Pact's primary provisions were later incorporated into the United Nations Charter of 1945, the bedrock of today's international order.

Disarmament negotiations ran in parallel with the attempt to abolish war. The Washington Naval Treaty of 1922 and the London Naval Treaties in the 1930s aimed to control the balance of naval fleets among the great powers and included provisions calling for the "progressive realization of general limitation and reduction of armaments". Within the context of the League, preparatory talks began on a "universal agreement on armament". It was in the context of these ultimately ill-fated conversations that, in 1927, the delegation of the Soviet Union made a dramatic call for "general and complete disarmament". There has been considerable debate among scholars, lawyers and diplomats—both at the time and ever since—whether the Soviet Union's proposal was earnest or simply a political flourish. However, the phrase took on a diplomatic life of its own—outliving the faltering talks of the 1920s and outgrowing its propagandistic Soviet origins—to be revived in the aftermath of the Second World War.

Disarmament, the United Nations and post-war liberal order

During the final stages of the Second World War, the Allies began planning for the post-war order, determined to ensure their security and not repeat the mistakes of the post–First World War Versailles peace. Within the Allies' political leadership, there were serious differences about how that would be achieved. There were pressures to revert to great power-dominated *realpolitik* along the lines of the Concert of Europe that had governed European relations during the nineteenth century. Joseph Stalin wanted to divide the world into great power "spheres of influence" and Winston Churchill and Charles de Gaulle were determined to re-establish the United Kingdom and France as colonial powers. Nevertheless, there was a strong interest in establishing liberal institutions of international order that would resolve disputes through diplomacy and law at the United Nations. The Universal Declaration of Human Rights of 1948, the Geneva Conventions of 1949, the Genocide Convention of 1951 and the Refugee Convention of 1951 provided the nascent outlines of what we now call "human security"—a recognition that States needed to limit the human costs of State violence.

While this history is rather familiar, it is less well-known that disarmament was a key element of the liberal vision, featured in the Atlantic Charter of 1941, which defined the Allies' goals in the Second World War. Disarmament was then institutionalized in the United Nations Charter. Article 11 grants the General Assembly the power to consider "principles governing disarmament and the regulation of armaments" and Article 26 gives the Security Council responsibility for "the establishment of a system for the regulation of armaments". Implementation of these and other collective security provisions were stunted by the ensuing cold war tensions. But the General Assembly, less controlled by the great powers, passed several early resolutions establishing a framework for international disarmament. Most notably, the body's first resolution called for the "elimination from national armaments of atomic weapons and all other major weapons adaptable to mass destruction". This was followed shortly by resolution 41 calling for the negotiation of treaties "governing the general regulation and reduction of armaments".

Indicative of the hopes of the post–Second World War era, the 1948 revolution in Costa Rica led to the abolition of their military forces and unilateral complete disarmament. While this national choice was replicated only in a few other States, Costa Rica has served as a counter-example to the conventional wisdom that disarmament is an unrealistic pipe dream.

General and complete disarmament becomes codified

In the standoff between the United States of America and the Soviet Union (and their respective blocs), disarmament and collective security initiatives struggled to overcome the emerging arms race. But rising tension in the 1950s increased public fears of another global war, now unwinnable given the advent of nuclear weapons. In 1955, a widely read manifesto by Albert Einstein, Bertrand Russell and eight other prominent intellectuals warned of the "peril" of nuclear war and demanded that the world's leaders agree to "renounce nuclear weapons as part of a general reduction of armaments". This inspired the Aldermaston protests in the United Kingdom, starting in 1958, in which thousands marched to a nuclear-weapon laboratory. The General Assembly responded to the growing public pressure with its resolution 1378, passed unanimously in 1959, which expressed "the hope that measures leading towards the goal of general and complete disarmament under effective international control will be worked out in detail and agreed upon in the shortest possible time".

The United States of America and the Soviet Union began a series of bilateral meetings, culminating in the McCloy-Zorin statement of 1961, a set of "jointly agreed principles" for an eventual treaty on GCD. It included the disbanding of armed forces, elimination of weapons of mass destruction and an end to military expenditures. Meanwhile, at their first summit in Belgrade, the Heads of State of the Non-Aligned Countries unanimously endorsed "general, complete and strictly internationally controlled disarmament". That September, United States President John F. Kennedy endorsed GCD in a rousing speech at the General Assembly. Now primarily remembered as a speech calling for the abolition of nuclear weapons, he told world leaders that GCD "must no longer be a slogan", as the McCloy-Zorin talks had now made it "a realistic plan". Inspired, the General Assembly endorsed the McCloy-Zorin principles, created an Eighteen-Nation Disarmament Committee, which later evolved into the Conference on Disarmament, and asked them to consider how to make GCD reality. It soon became clear that bridging differences over the practicalities of achieving such a grand vision would be challenging. The United States State Department issued a white paper, *Freedom from War: The United States Program for General and Complete Disarmament in a Peaceful World*, which today seems stunningly ambitious, calling for the disbanding of national armed forces and elimination of "all armaments". However, the subtle grammar of its title suggests that GCD is something that would happen "in a peaceful world"—that is, in conditions where peace already exists. This was interpreted as disingenuous by the Soviet Union and, in both superpowers, few of the military elite were really prepared to accept comprehensive demobilization. Nevertheless, GCD had become the expressed consensus commitment of the international community.

The broad global acceptance of GCD as an achievable goal in 1961 was perhaps its high watermark, as the Cuban Missile Crisis of 1962 brought the superpowers to the brink of nuclear war. The renewed danger made progress on arms negotiations not only more urgent but also more difficult. As a result, the United States and the Soviet Union began earnest negotiations on nuclear weapons but eventually abandoned pursuit of a more general and complete agreement in favour of "partial measures". These included the Hotline Agreement and Partial Test Ban Treaty, both in 1963. Over the rest of the cold war, the superpowers moved away from the paradigm of multilateral disarmament to one of bilateral "arms control", focused on limiting the numbers of large-scale strategic weapons. GCD remained a rhetorical goal, however, and was written into the preamble of the Partial Test Ban Treaty.

Meanwhile, frustration with the lack of progress towards nuclear disarmament by the superpowers spurred smaller States to seek alternative pathways to disarmament. In the General Assembly, they called for a convention prohibiting nuclear weapons in 1963 (resolution 1909 (XVIII)). Latin American States moved forward on establishing a nuclear-weapon-free zone in 1967, which they described as "not an end in themselves but rather a means for achieving general and complete disarmament at a later stage". The global peace movement was also revived in the 1960s, catalysed by fears of nuclear war and instability in the newly decolonizing countries.

Growing political and diplomatic pressure on the nuclear powers led them to the negotiating table, resulting in the "Grand Bargain" in 1968 of the Treaty on the Non-Proliferation of Nuclear Weapons (NPT), in which non-nuclear-weapon States agreed not to acquire nuclear weapons in exchange for access to peaceful nuclear energy and disarmament. While often cited only in the context of nuclear disarmament policymaking, the Treaty's article VI actually established a legal obligation on the States parties—now almost the entire membership of the United Nations—to "pursue negotiations in good faith ... on a treaty on general and complete disarmament under strict and effective international control".

In the following three decades, every major multilateral arms control treaty—including the Biological Weapons Convention of 1972, the Environmental Modification Convention of 1977, the Convention on Certain Conventional Weapons of 1981, the Chemical Weapons Convention of 1992, the Comprehensive-Test-Ban Treaty of 1996 and the African Nuclear-Weapon-Free Zone Treaty of 1996—described itself (though only in the preamble) as one step towards the ultimate goal of GCD. However, no serious deliberations on GCD itself have taken place since 1961 and article VI of the NPT remains the only legally binding GCD provision. Indeed, the Final Document of the 1978 special session of the General Assembly devoted to disarmament criticized the focus on partial measures as having "done little to bring the world closer to the goal of general and complete disarmament", allowing the arms race to continue unabated.

What happened to the general and complete disarmament agenda?

A rarely acknowledged irony of the post–cold war era is that it ushered in a moment when the world came closest to achieving GCD but, simultaneously, the concept was discursively marginalized and discredited as "unrealistic". Analysis by Neil Cooper has shown that, despite exponential population growth, post–cold war military reductions have cut numbers of troops close to the levels sufficient for national safety and international peace operations that were discussed in the GCD negotiations in the 1950s and 1960s. But one now rarely hears of GCD in diplomatic circles, except by nuclear powers trying to obfuscate their nuclear disarmament obligations (by tying them to a distant day of world peace) or as a punch line. Indicative is the Treaty on Conventional Armed Forces in Europe (CFE) of 1989. It is one of the most successful post–cold war arms reduction agreements, achieving a widespread demilitarization of Europe, but it does not refer to GCD.

Global civil society has reengaged with disarmament, seeking to renew and expand the norms against inhumane weapons by persuading the majority of the world's States to ban antipersonnel landmines in 1997 and cluster munitions in 2008. This "humanitarian disarmament" movement also played a major role in pushing for the Arms Trade Treaty (ATT) of 2013, which established global regulations on the trade and transfer of conventional weapons. However, the humanitarian disarmament advocacy has implicitly distanced itself from GCD by focusing on limiting particularly odious methods of warfare rather than seeking a holistic settlement on arms. None of the humanitarian disarmament treaties—neither the ATT nor the landmine and cluster munition bans—mention GCD.

The sort of comprehensive disarmament envisioned by the concept of GCD—reducing security forces and arsenals to no more than is needed for national safety—can now be talked about in policy circles only as something that is "done to" a former conflict zone, usually in the Global South. Many United Nations peace operations in conflict-affected developing countries have a "disarmament, demobilization and reintegration" (DDR) component. But this is conceived as a corrective programme for deviant, "war-torn" spaces, not as a general and global obligation incumbent on all States, including the great military powers.

Besides this discursive relegation of GCD, there remain several key challenges to achieving the goal of GCD:

- *Stalled nuclear disarmament.* Reductions to nuclear arsenals have slowed in recent years and the nuclear-weapon States have embarked on expensive "modernization" programmes that may extend the threat of nuclear war for decades. Achieving GCD will thus depend on undercutting the legitimacy of nuclear weapons as the perceived cornerstone of great power security structures.

- *Asymmetries in the global military balance.* According to the Stockholm International Peace Research Institute, 34 per cent of the world's military spending is by the United States of America and 28 per cent is by the next top five military powers. The primary focus of disarmament must therefore be on those who have the most arms.

- *Qualitative improvements in weapons.* The quantitative reductions in global military forces after the cold war coincided with innovations in weaponry, particularly in information and communications technology. This created new capabilities even as some arsenals shrank. New technologies such as the armed drone have destabilized international legal norms on the use of force outside declared conflict zones.

- *Globalization of the political economy of war.* The complex processes of globalization have transformed armed conflict by making weapons more easily available. In fact, the emptying of cold war weapons stocks, particularly in Eastern Europe, in many cases redirected small arms to conflicts in the Global South. The informalization and privatization of violence has proliferated the kinds of armed actors and complicated chains of command and accountability.

- *Creaking disarmament machinery.* The diplomatic systems set up to achieve GCD are under strain, marginalized by ministries of foreign affairs and defence. They are dominated by the great powers and marginalize the concerns of small States, civil society and those most affected by violence.

Whither general and complete disarmament?

In 2007 United Nations Secretary-General Ban Ki-moon reaffirmed GCD as "the ultimate strategic goal" of United Nations disarmament efforts. In a landmark 2014 speech in Moscow, United Nations disarmament chief Angela Kane decried that people "forget" GCD as a codified goal of multilateral diplomacy and called on the United States and the Russian Federation to "revive interest" in "comprehensive disarmament". Much of the world's military force levels are actually in compliance with an admittedly restrictive definition of GCD, which allows arsenals no larger than what is needed for national safety and meeting international obligations. The discursive dismissal of GCD as "unrealistic" is thus less a description of actual force levels than a convenient excuse that functions to undermine critique of great power militarism.

Diplomatic efforts to define and achieve GCD have perhaps left too much of the initiative to the very States most responsible for global overarmament. But just because the great powers have the most arms does not mean they are necessarily the only credible agents of disarmament. The nuclear-weapon-free zones in Africa, Latin America, South-East Asia and the South Pacific offer a model of how small and middle powers can codify their lack of armament. States from such zones have played an important role in the humanitarian initiative on nuclear weapons, which aims to move nuclear disarmament policy forward with or without the nuclear-weapon States. Drawing on this history, one could imagine the negotiation of regional GCD zones.

Reviewing the history of GCD reminds us that it was taken seriously by "serious people" and even written into international law. It allows us to pay attention to a concept that haunts the edges of our conventional wisdom about global security policy. The point is not to indulge in nostalgic "what if" counterfactuals, but to have the past challenge our present complacency and reintroduce GCD as a "thinkable thought". This is the great contribution of the proposal by the Strategic Concept for Removal of Arms and Proliferation (SCRAP) project at SOAS, University of London, outlined in more detail elsewhere in this volume. SCRAP has been deliberately framed "as a provocation to those who believed that multilateral and comprehensive disarmament, both conventional and nuclear, was impossible". In presenting a plan for GCD rooted in existing precedents (such as the CFE Treaty), it demands a more substantive response than the usual condescending dismissal of GCD. Given that the proposal of United Nations Sustainable Development Goal 16 is to "promote peace and inclusive societies", it is time to rehabilitate GCD discursively as a primary aim of multilateral diplomacy.

Bibliography

Bolton, M. (2015). General and Complete Disarmament. NPT News in Review, 13 (13): 10.

Cooper, N. (2006). Putting Disarmament back in the frame. *Review of International Studies*, 32: 353-376.

Curnow, R., Kaldor, M., McLean, M., Robinson, J., and Shepherd, P. (1976). General and complete disarmament: A systems-analysis approach. *Futures*, 8 (5), 384-396.

Jonas, D. S. (2011). General and Complete Disarmament: Not Just for Nuclear Weapons States Anymore. *Georgetown Journal of International Law*, 43, 587.

Kant, I. (1795). *Perpetual Peace: A Philosophical Sketch* [online]. Available from http://www.constitution.org/kant/perpeace.htm (accessed 23 August 2015).

Kane, A. (2014). Outlook for the 2015 NPT Review Conference and Beyond: The Roles of the Russian Federation and the United States [online]. Available from http://scrapweapons.com/wp-content/uploads/2015/01/Kane-Remarks-2014-Moscow.pdf (accessed 23 August 2015).

Kennedy, J. F. (1961). JFK Address at U.N. General Assembly, 25 September 1961 [online]. Available from http://www.jfklibrary.org/Asset-Viewer/DOPIN64xJUGRKgd HJ9NfgQ.aspx (accessed 23 August 2015).

Mazower, M. (2013). *Governing the World: The History of an Idea, 1815 to the Present.* New York, Penguin Books.

McCloy, J. J. and Zorin, V. (1961). McCloy-Zorin Accords [online]. Available from http://www.nuclearfiles.org/menu/key-issues/ nuclear-weapons/issues/arms-control-disarmament/mccloy-zorin-accords_1961-09-20.htm (accessed 23 August 2015).

Russell, B. et al. (1955). The Russell-Einstein Manifesto [online]. Available from http://pugwash.org/1955/07/09/statement-manifesto/ (accessed 23 August 2015).

Rydell, R. (2009). Nuclear disarmament and general and complete disarmament. In *The Challenge of Abolishing Nuclear Weapons*, D. Kreiger (ed.). New Brunswick, Transaction Publishers, 227-242.

United States Department of State (1961). Freedom from War: The United States Program for General and Complete Disarmament in a Peaceful World. Washington, D.C., United States Department of State.

SCRAP (n.d.). Strategic Concept for Removal of Arms and Proliferation [online]. Available from http://www.cisd.soas. ac.uk/Editor/assets/scrap%201.4%20web%20version.pdf (accessed 23 August 2015).

Stockholm International Peace Research Institute (2015). Trends in World Military Expenditure, 2014 [online]. Available from http://books.sipri.org/product_info?c_product_id=496 (accessed 23 August 2015).

Legal aspects of general and complete disarmament

John Burroughs
Executive Director, Lawyers Committee on Nuclear Policy
Director, International Association of Lawyers Against Nuclear
Arms, United Nations Office

General and complete disarmament (GCD), especially nuclear disarmament, is embedded in the DNA of the United Nations. Based on the role of GCD in the United Nations and the treaty obligation to negotiate a GCD treaty contained in article VI of the Treaty on the Non-Proliferation of Nuclear Weapons (NPT), GCD is clearly a global political aim of the highest order; beyond that, it is arguably an obligation of customary international law applying to all States, including those outside the NPT. In view of the practice of States since the NPT was negotiated, the fulfilment of the obligation of nuclear disarmament articulated in NPT article VI is not legally contingent on the achievement of GCD. However, the inclusion in article VI of the objectives of both nuclear disarmament and GCD underlines the practical, mutually reinforcing relationship between nuclear disarmament and control and the elimination of other strategic weapon systems.

United Nations

Article 11 of the United Nations Charter provides that the General Assembly may make recommendations to United Nations Member States and the Security Council with regard to the "principles governing disarmament and the regulation of armaments". Article 26 provides that the Security Council is responsible for formulating plans to be submitted to Member States "for the establishment of a system for the regulation of armaments". The Security Council has not fulfilled Article 26, but the General Assembly has vigorously exercised its power under Article 11.

In its very first resolution, unanimously adopted in 1946 five months after the United States nuclear bombings of Hiroshima and Nagasaki, the General Assembly established the Atomic Energy Commission to make specific proposals for, among other things, "the elimination from national armaments of atomic weapons and of all other major weapons adaptable to mass destruction".[1] This effort failed, but the General Assembly persevered, placing nuclear disarmament in the wider context of what came to be known as general and complete disarmament. Thus, in resolution 808 (IX) A, unanimously adopted in 1954, the Assembly concluded

> that a further effort should be made to reach agreement on comprehensive and co-ordinated proposals to be embodied in a draft international disarmament convention providing for:
>
> (a)　The regulation, limitation and major reduction of all armed forces and all conventional armaments;
>
> (b)　The total prohibition of the use and manufacture of nuclear weapons and weapons of mass destruction of every type, together with the conversion of existing stocks of nuclear weapons for peaceful purposes;
>
> (c)　The establishment of effective international control, through a control organ with rights, powers and functions adequate to guarantee the effective observance of the agreed reductions of all armament and armed forces and the prohibition of nuclear and other weapons of mass destruction, and to ensure the use of atomic energy for peaceful purposes only.[2]

This approach informed United Nations efforts in the Disarmament Commission and other bodies until negotiations

---

[1]　General Assembly resolution 1 (I) of 24 January 1946.
[2]　General Assembly resolution 808 (IX) A of 4 November 1954.

on the NPT began in earnest in 1965. Notable landmarks along the way include the following:

- General Assembly resolution 1378 (XIV), co-sponsored by all United Nations Member States and adopted unanimously in 1959, which proclaimed general and complete disarmament as a goal and put it permanently on the United Nations agenda;[3]

- A "Joint statement of agreed principles for disarmament negotiations" by the Soviet Union and the United States put forward on 20 September 1961;[4]

- General Assembly resolution 1722 (XVI), unanimously adopted on 20 December 1961, which recommended negotiations upon general and complete disarmament based upon the United States–Soviet agreed principles in a body known as the Eighteen-Nation Disarmament Committee (ENDC);[5]

- Negotiations in the ENDC from 1962 to 1965 on proposals by the Soviet Union and the United States for a treaty on general and complete disarmament. Those proposals differed greatly in detail, but in general envisaged drastic, staged reductions in troop numbers and conventional arms; reduction and eventual elimination of nuclear, biological and chemical weapons; control of the process of disarmament by an international organ; establishment (United States, which called for eventual creation of a United Nations peace force) or enhancement (Soviet Union) of United Nations capabilities to resolve conflicts and to keep the peace.[6]

---

[3] General Assembly resolution 1378 (XIV) of 20 November 1959.
[4] A/4879.
[5] General Assembly resolution 1722 (XVI) of 20 December 1961.
[6] See *The United Nations and Disarmament: 1945-1970* (United Nations publication, Sales No. E.76.IX.1), pp. 91-102 and appendices II and III.

Key elements of GCD as conceived in the first two decades of the United Nations are that it is comprehensive, encompassing all major weapons and armed forces; implemented through staged and balanced reductions; subject to verification by an international organ or organs; and accompanied by strengthening or creating mechanisms for resolving conflict and keeping the peace.

As Randy Rydell has explained,[7] after efforts to negotiate a GCD treaty in the 1950s and early 1960s failed, the ENDC, its successors, including today's Conference on Disarmament, and States have generally focused on partial measures, such as the NPT, the Comprehensive Nuclear-Test-Ban Treaty and the conventions on biological and chemical weapons.

Nonetheless, general and complete disarmament has remained the overarching objective. It was strongly reasserted by the seminal 1978 special session of the General Assembly on disarmament. In the Final Document,[8] the Assembly identified general and complete disarmament under effective international control as the "ultimate objective"[9] and gave first priority in negotiations to nuclear weapons, followed by other weapons of mass destruction; conventional weapons, including any which may be deemed to be excessively injurious or to have indiscriminate effects; and the reduction of armed forces.[10] One important element of the GCD approach, the establishment of international organs for verification and monitoring of disarmament, has been partially realized, notably by the Organisation for the Prohibition of Chemical Weapons created by the Chemical Weapons Convention.

---

[7] Randy Rydell, "Nuclear Disarmament and General and Complete Disarmament," in David Krieger, ed., *The Challenge of Abolishing Nuclear Weapons* (New Brunswick and London: Transaction Publishers, 2009), esp. pp. 233-234.

[8] "Final Document of the Tenth Special Session of the General Assembly" in General Assembly resolution S-10/2 of 30 June 1978.

[9] Ibid., para. 19.

[10] Ibid., para. 45.

Article VI of the Treaty on the Non-Proliferation of Nuclear Weapons

Article VI of the NPT provides:

Each of the Parties to the Treaty undertakes to pursue negotiations in good faith on effective measures relating to cessation of the nuclear arms race at an early date and to nuclear disarmament, and on a treaty on general and complete disarmament under strict and effective international control.

The three prongs of article VI concern cessation of the nuclear arms race at an early date, nuclear disarmament and general and complete disarmament.

Cessation of the nuclear arms race was to be accomplished by measures including banning production of fissile materials for nuclear weapons, banning tests of nuclear explosives and capping nuclear arsenals. Its early achievement was to facilitate the reduction and elimination of nuclear weapons.

Nuclear disarmament was to be accomplished by measures to reduce and eliminate nuclear weapons. Shortly after the NPT was signed, the Geneva-based Eighteen-Nation Disarmament Committee, the precursor of today's Conference on Disarmament, under United States and Soviet leadership, adopted an agenda whose first item was listed under a heading taken from article VI:

1.   Further effective measures relating to the cessation of nuclear arms race at an early date and to nuclear disarmament. Under this heading, members may wish to discuss measures dealing with the cessation of testing, the non-use of nuclear weapons, the cessation of production of fissionable materials for weapons use, the cessation of manufacture of weapons and reduction and subsequent elimination of nuclear stockpiles, nuclear-free zones, etc.

2.   Non-nuclear measures. Under this heading, members may wish to discuss chemical and bacteriological warfare, regional arms limitations, etc.

3.   Other collateral measures. Under this heading, members may wish to discuss prevention of an arms race on the sea-bed, etc.

4.   General and complete disarmament under strict and effective international control.[11]

Item 1 encapsulated multilateral measures contemplated during negotiation of the NPT for the fulfilment of the article VI obligations as to cessation of the nuclear arms race and nuclear disarmament. It includes reduction and subsequent *elimination* of nuclear stockpiles as an *effective measure*. General and complete disarmament was a separate agenda item.

General and complete disarmament was to be accomplished by negotiation of a treaty on GCD. The NPT preamble indicates that a GCD treaty was to encompass the elimination of nuclear weapons, referring to "elimination from national arsenals of nuclear weapons and the means of their delivery pursuant to a Treaty on general and complete disarmament under strict and effective international control". However, as just noted, it was also understood at the outset that "effective measures ... relating to nuclear disarmament" include those accomplishing the elimination of nuclear weapons. Moreover, the practice of States since the NPT was negotiated has been to adopt weapons-specific treaties to advance GCD. Under article 31 of the Vienna Convention on the Law of Treaties, such practice is a relevant factor in treaty interpretation.

---

[11] Eighteen-Nation Committee on Disarmament, Final Verbatim Record of the 390th Meeting, document ENDC/PV.390. Available from http://quod.lib.umich.edu/e/endc/4918260.0390.001?rgn=main;view=full text (accessed 3 August 2016).

When the NPT was negotiated, a GCD treaty was understood, as earlier explained, as a comprehensive agreement at a minimum providing for the reduction and elimination of nuclear weapons and other weapons of mass destruction, the limitation and reduction of armed forces and conventional armaments, and the establishment of effective international control through an organ or organs, and at a maximum additionally enhancing conflict prevention mechanisms and providing for demilitarization to the point of abolishing national armed forces and establishing a United Nations peace force. Subsequent to the entry into force of the NPT, the practice of States has been to negotiate separate conventions on prohibition and elimination of weapons of mass destruction, with the Biological Weapons Convention of 1972 and the Chemical Weapons Convention of 1993. The International Court of Justice (ICJ) took note of this practice, stating in its advisory opinion in 1996 on nuclear weapons that the "pattern until now has been for weapons of mass destruction to be declared illegal by specific instruments".[12] The practice of States has also been to negotiate separate treaties on other types of weapons, such as anti-personnel landmines and cluster munitions. These matters are mostly considered by the General Assembly under the rubric "General and complete disarmament" and all are considered under the heading "Disarmament".[13]

In light of this history, a comprehensive convention on nuclear disarmament (or instruments to the same end) would, like the conventions on chemical and biological weapons, partially fulfil the general and complete disarmament prong of article VI. The NPT Review Conference Final Documents in 1995, 2000 and 2010 accord with this view. Notably, in the

---

[12] *Advisory Opinion of 8 July 1996 on the Legality of the Threat or Use of Nuclear Weapons, I.C.J. Reports 1996*, p. 248 (hereafter "Nuclear Weapons Advisory Opinion"), para. 57.

[13] See "Organization of the seventieth regular session of the General Assembly, adoption of the agenda and allocation of items", A/70/250, pp. 20-23.

practical steps towards implementing article VI adopted at the 2000 NPT Review Conference, step 6, "An unequivocal undertaking by the nuclear-weapon States to accomplish the total elimination of their nuclear arsenals ...", is set out separately from step 11, "Reaffirmation that the ultimate objective of the efforts of States in the disarmament process is general and complete disarmament under effective international control".[14]

In sum, the elimination of nuclear weapons would fulfil the second prong of article VI concerning effective measures relating to nuclear disarmament and partially fulfil the objective of general and complete disarmament set out in the third prong. The ICJ formulation of the nuclear disarmament obligation is in harmony with this interpretation of article VI. The Court unanimously concluded that "There exists an obligation to pursue in good faith and bring to a conclusion negotiations on nuclear disarmament in all its aspects under strict and effective international control."[15] The obligation so stated encompasses both the second component of article VI relating to nuclear disarmament and the third component relating to general and complete disarmament "under strict and effective international control".

Customary international law

The ICJ formulation of the obligation to negotiate nuclear disarmament, "There exists an obligation ...", and its underlying analysis virtually compel the reading that the obligation applies universally, including to States not party to the NPT; that is, that the obligation is one of customary international law. Thus United Nations Secretary-General Ban Ki-moon characterized the Court's approach as follows:

---

[14] NPT/CONF.2000/28 (Parts I and II), pp. 14-15. Available from http://www.un.org/disarmament/WMD/Nuclear/2000-NPT/pdf/FD-Part1and2.pdf (accessed 3 August 2016).

[15] Nuclear Weapons Advisory Opinion, para. 105(2)F.

No country disputes the desirability of achieving a nuclear-weapon-free world. After all, this was the very first objective identified by the United Nations General Assembly. The universal acceptance of this goal led the International Court of Justice to determine that the disarmament obligation transcends any treaty and is a requirement under customary international law.[16]

In its analysis, the Court first notes that "the vast majority of the international community" is bound by the NPT,[17] implicitly invoking the doctrine that customary international law can arise out of multilateral treaties with widespread participation. Moreover, the Court observes,

> Virtually the whole of this community appears moreover to have been involved when resolutions of the United Nations General Assembly concerning nuclear disarmament have repeatedly been unanimously adopted. Indeed, any realistic search for general and complete disarmament, especially nuclear disarmament, necessitates the co-operation of all States.[18]

General Assembly resolutions, when very widely supported, can provide evidence of customary international law. Based on these and other factors, and on the ICJ opinion itself, there is a powerful case that the obligation to negotiate nuclear disarmament is customary in nature. That proposition is

---

[16] United Nations Secretary-General, message to the Vienna Conference on the Humanitarian Impact of Nuclear Weapons, Vienna, 8 December 2014. Available from http://www.bmeia.gv.at/fileadmin/user_upload/Zentrale/Aussenpolitik/Abruestung/HINW14/HINW14_Message_from_UN_Secretary_General.pdf (accessed 3 August 2016).

[17] Nuclear Weapons Advisory Opinion, para. 100.

[18] Ibid.

now being tested in the Marshall Islands' current cases in the International Court of Justice.[19]

Essentially the same arguments support the view that the obligation to negotiate general and complete disarmament is customary in nature. That obligation is contained in article VI of the NPT. Further, as explained at the outset, General Assembly resolutions and the Final Document of the 1978 special session set GCD as a prime objective of the international community, consistently with articles 11 and 26 of the United Nations Charter. It is beyond doubt, in any case, that there is a well-established political norm enjoining negotiations relating to GCD.

Practical importance of general and complete disarmament

As a *matter of law*, the obligation to negotiate the elimination of nuclear weapons is independent of the obligation to negotiate general and complete disarmament. However, the following point strongly to a *practical*, mutually reinforcing relationship between nuclear disarmament and other weapons control efforts: early General Assembly resolutions; article VI itself; the flurry of related negotiations at the end of the cold war on nuclear reductions, the Chemical Weapons Convention

---

[19] In its cases against India and Pakistan, the Marshall Islands claims that those States are failing to comply with obligations of nuclear disarmament arising under customary international law. In its case against the United Kingdom, the Marshall Islands claims that the United Kingdom is failing to comply with obligations of nuclear disarmament arising under both the NPT and customary international law. The Marshall Islands also filed applications against the six other nuclear-armed States; however, unlike India, Pakistan and the United Kingdom, they have not accepted the compulsory jurisdiction of the Court and have not accepted the Marshall Islands' invitation to come before the Court voluntarily. The applications and other pleadings in the India, Pakistan and United Kingdom cases can be viewed at the website of the ICJ, available from www.icj-cij.org. All nine applications are available from www.nuclearzero.org.

and the Treaty on Conventional Armed Forces in Europe; and the current impasse in nuclear arms reductions arising in part from the United States push for missile defences and its growing strategic conventional capabilities. To succeed in abolishing nuclear arms, and for other compelling reasons as well, a renewed focus on general and complete disarmament is imperative.

Reconciling national security and general and complete disarmament

Marc Finaud
Senior Programme Advisor
Emerging Security Challenges Programme
Geneva Centre for Security Policy

The concept of general and complete disarmament

As explained earlier in this volume,[1] the concept of general and complete disarmament (GCD), which crystalized during the cold war, is reflected in article VI of the Treaty on the Non-Proliferation of Nuclear Weapons (NPT). According to that key provision, all States parties are under the obligation "to pursue negotiations in good faith" not only on "effective measures relating to cessation of the nuclear arms race at an early date and to nuclear disarmament" but *also* "on a treaty on general and complete disarmament under strict and effective international control" and there is no conditionality whatsoever between the former and the latter.

Despite progress in implementation of this dual obligation, important gaps remain: few treaties led to the actual elimination of nuclear weapons; the only multilateral agreements on nuclear weapons[2] apply not to disarmament but mainly to non-proliferation; no disarmament instrument is completely universal and some States parties are non-compliant with their commitments; some critical armaments are not covered, such as missiles, which can be both conventional weapons and delivery vehicles of weapons of mass destruction; and military

---

[1] See particularly the chapter in this volume by Matthew Bolton entitled "Time for a discursive rehabilitation: A brief history of general and complete disarmament".

[2] Partial Test Ban Treaty of 1963, Treaty on the Non-Proliferation of Nuclear Weapons of 1968, Sea-bed Treaty of 1971 and Comprehensive-Test-Ban Treaty of 1996.

expenditures and arms transfers continue to increase, often stimulated by the defence industry and/or State suppliers.

Admittedly, disarmament cannot occur in a political vacuum and it is only a means to an end: *national and international security*. In that respect, the United Nations Security Council has identified the key objective in its historic resolution 1887 (2009), unanimously adopted at the level of Heads of State or Government in 2009 "to seek a safer world for all and to *create the conditions* [emphasis added] for a world without nuclear weapons, in accordance with the goals of the [NPT], in a way that promotes international stability, and based on the principle of undiminished security for all".

Some interpret this commitment in a restrictive manner: unless some security conditions are created, there can be no abolition of nuclear weapons. Additionally, this can only be done if "stability" and "undiminished security" are maintained, which is coded language for preserving retaliatory capabilities, opposing antiballistic missile defence and the weaponization of outer space and rejecting unilateral disarmament measures.[3] But this interpretation distorts the initial goal of the NPT; the conditions for a world without nuclear weapons should not be *preconditions*. Indeed, in the words of Angela Kane, the former High Representative of the United Nations for Disarmament Affairs,

> There are several problems with the alternative approach of insisting on preconditions. One of them is that the list of such conditions is open-ended, and we have seen a cascade of conditions that allegedly must be satisfied before nuclear disarmament is "possible". Some observers demand world peace. Some say all regional disputes must first be solved. Some demand a solution to the problem of war and armed conflict. Some demand a definitive end to all

---

[3] Ray Acheson, "Whose NPT?", *NPT News in Review*, vol. 13, no. 7, 11 May 2015.

proliferation and terrorist risks. Some call for an end to missile defence. Some require a ban on space weapons. Some even call for world government. Etcetera.[4]

Indeed, by agreeing to act in order to create conditions for a world without nuclear weapons, the nuclear-weapon States are undeniably bound to address all the other issues that have been used as reasons for delaying nuclear disarmament, such as the other challenges to their national security.[5]

The Westphalian notion of national security

When the concept of GCD was elaborated and the NPT was negotiated, the Westphalian notion of State was prevailing and the idea of security was narrowly associated with *national security*—meaning, for some (often non-democratic) States, protection of the Government or the ruling regime—and the State was defined as the only entity with the "legitimacy to use physical force in a given territory", as Max Weber did.[6] In this political and legal system resulting from centuries of history, national security primarily amounts to protecting territorial integrity or sovereignty from external threats from other States and responding to such threats mostly by military means.

The doctrine of *nuclear deterrence* was predicated on a *zero-sum-game* approach: the security of one State relied on the

---

[4] Angela Kane, High Representative for Disarmament Affairs, "Creating the Conditions and Building the Framework for a Nuclear Weapons-Free World", opening remarks at the luncheon discussion hosted by Middle Powers Initiative and the Permanent Mission of Germany to the United Nations, New York, 10 October 2012.

[5] For more discussion of this idea, see David Atwood and Emily J. Munro, eds. "Security in a World without Nuclear Weapons," *GCSP Report*, 2013. Available from http://www.gcsp.ch/News-Knowledge/Publications/Security-in-a-World-without-Nuclear-Weapons-Visions-and-Challenges (accessed 5 August 2016).

[6] Daniel Warner, *An Ethic of Responsibility in International Relations*, Lynne Rienner, publishers, 1991, pp. 9-10.

insecurity of other States. It was and still is in fact based on two major, intrinsically related factors: *fear* and *power*. Nuclear powers nurture fear from potential enemies and rely on the fear of potential destruction that would be inflicted on their enemies as a response to aggression by the latter. Even when the actual risk of aggression tends to disappear (like at the end of the cold war), nuclear-weapon States find in the alleged power conferred upon them by nuclear weapons a new reason for maintaining them.

Nowadays, power results less from the traditional instruments of State power, such as military might epitomized by nuclear weapons and more from economic and/or demographic dynamism, capacity for technological innovation, digital transformation and intellectual influence, qualified by Joseph Nye as *soft power*.[7] The whole notion of security has thus evolved to encompass human security—that is, the security of individuals and communities implying protection from complex, interrelated threats originating both beyond national borders (such as climate change, pandemics, terrorism, uncontrolled migration, organized crime, financial crises, uncontrolled migration and uneven access to energy, food, water, or natural resources) and occasionally from people's own Governments when they perpetrate mass violations of human rights. Needless to say, none of those threats can be deterred or combated with nuclear weapons. Such weapons are thus increasingly condemned to irrelevance.

The comprehensive security approach offered by general and complete disarmament

One advantage of reviving the concept of GCD would be to offer a comprehensive and holistic view of all the current and potential categories of weapons likely to be used for offensive or destabilizing rather than defensive purposes, as well as

---

[7] See Pierre Buhler, *La puissance au XXIe siècle* (Paris: CNRS Éditions, 2011).

all the interrelationships between them. It could defeat the argument consisting in refusing to deal with one category of weapons because other categories are deemed more threatening or destabilizing. A negotiation on all those categories would also allow all sorts of mutual concessions and gains across the spectrum of security tools.

Eventually, the GCD approach would also allow the United Nations Security Council to finally fulfil one of its key roles according to Article 26 of the United Nations Charter— the "establishment of a system of *regulation of armaments* [emphasis added]" "in order to promote the establishment and maintenance of international peace and security with the least diversion for armaments of the world's human and economic resources". This is in sum what GCD would in fact amount to: ensuring for all States defensive capabilities at the lowest possible level of armaments on the basis of a cooperative (or "win-win") approach of security that would release resources[8] to address the transnational non-military threats to the whole world.

Indeed, GCD would be one of the best ways to implement the paradigm of *cooperative security*, as opposed to competitive security or zero-sum-game approaches, which characterize nuclear deterrence. The concept is not a utopian dream. It has underpinned the whole Helsinki process put into place during the cold war by a divided Europe and remains the foundation of the Organization for Security and Cooperation in Europe (OSCE). In 1982 the Olaf Palme Commission put disarmament at the centre of a common, cooperative security framework.[9] After the cold war, the United States and the Russian Federation collaborated in the Cooperative Threat Reduction Program, the

---

[8] For instance, the current total United Nations annual budget, including peacekeeping operations (i.e., $13.98 billion) could be funded by the equivalent of only *three days* of the annual military expenditure of the world (i.e., $1,776 billion).

[9] See *Bulletin of the Atomic Scientists*, August/September 1982, vol. 38, issue 7, p. 65.

purpose of which was to "secure and dismantle [weapons of mass destruction] and their associated infrastructure in former Soviet Union states".[10] Regrettably, that programme, which had allowed the dismantlement of hundreds of nuclear or chemical weapons and nuclear-powered submarines, the training of staff and the securing of many facilities containing weapons material, was recently terminated by the Russian Federation.[11]

If nuclear-armed States are so concerned about "strategic stability", that realist concept would be better served by a series of legally binding and verifiable disarmament agreements than by an uncontrolled arms race open to more and more emerging States that would add destabilizing factors to the already volatile, unpredictable and multidimensional security environment. Rather than simplifying the security dilemma, this trend would complicate strategic calculations, favour escalations, enhance risks of confrontation and divert even more resources from economic and social development to wasteful military spending.

---

[10] See Defense Threat Reduction Agency, "Cooperative threat reducation". Available from http://web.archive.org/web/20070927215354/http://www.dtra.mil/oe/ctr/programs/ (accessed 5 August 2016).

[11] Bryan Bender, "Russia Ends US Nuclear Security Alliance", *Boston Globe*, 19 January 2015.

Part 2

Overcoming contemporary challenges to general and complete disarmament

Creating disarmament synergies: The general and complete disarmament multiplier

Randy Rydell
Executive Advisor, Mayors for Peace
Senior Political Affairs Officer (retired),
United Nations Office for Disarmament Affairs

There are few concepts as badly misunderstood in the disarmament and arms control literature as "general and complete disarmament under effective international control" or GCD. To some ill-informed observers, GCD is prima facie unacceptable because of its utopian connotations: it implies the elimination of literally every weapon, of all types, everywhere. Working from this false premise, such critics typically conclude that GCD is "unrealistic"—or at best a concept to be viewed as an "ultimate goal", to be achieved only when all other challenges are resolved first. Even the United Nations treats GCD as an "ultimate goal".[1]

This essay takes a different approach, one that identifies GCD as an ensemble of institutional, legal and political constructs that bring together the various strands of disarmament, arms control and non-proliferation into a coherent framework. It is an integrating tool, a means for making sense of how the act of eliminating certain types of weaponry (e.g., weapons of mass destruction) relates to other dimensions of international peace and security. This unique function of GCD gives it the potential to multiply manyfold the benefits that can be achieved by pursuing disarmament, arms control and non-proliferation in isolation and on a piecemeal basis. The whole of GCD is larger than the sum of its parts.

---

[1] It is so designated in the Final Document of the first special session of the General Assembly on disarmament in 1978.

General and complete disarmament and the "Dirty Dozen"

For over seven decades, disarmament's detractors around the world have relied on a surprisingly limited set of premises to reach their familiar conclusion that nuclear disarmament—let alone "general and complete" disarmament—is a fool's errand. Speaking in 2010 as the United Nations Under-Secretary-General for Disarmament Affairs, Sergio Duarte distilled these arguments down to an even 12 that he called the "Dirty Dozen".[2] These arguments continue to reappear in contemporary diatribes against nuclear disarmament and comprise the following mantra:

1. Disarmament is utopian and impractical.

2. Disarmament is dangerous, undermining nuclear alliances.

3. Disarmament is a lower priority than non-proliferation or counter-terrorism.

4. Disarmament is irrelevant—certain States or non-state actors will never comply.

5. Disarmament is best seen as only a distant goal.

6. Disarmament deprives us of nuclear weapons to keep the order and deter war.

7. Disarmament is unenforceable.

---

[2] Sergio Duarte, lecture at Chautauqua Institution, Chautauqua, New York, 19 July 2010. Available from https://unoda-web.s3-accelerate. amazonaws.com/wp-content/uploads/assets/HomePage/HR/docs/2010/ 2010July19Chautauqua.pdf (accessed 4 August 2016). A typical example of this perspective is found in Bradley A. Thayer and Thomas M. Skypek, "Reaffirming the Utility of Nuclear Weapons," *Parameters*, Winter/Spring 2013, p. 41, where the authors asserted that "nuclear disarmament is an unpleasant dream that would jeopardize US security, make the world safe for conventional war, and undermine global stability."

8. Disarmament is unverifiable, as cheating will occur and go undetected.

9. Disarmament would open the way for conventional wars.

10. Disarmament would lead to an expensive increase in conventional arms.

11. Disarmament should only apply to States that are unreliable.

12. Disarmament ignores the reality that nuclear weapons cannot be disinvented.

These assertions reveal a startling unfamiliarity with GCD, a concept that has come to recognize the synergies of pursuing simultaneously the elimination of weapons of mass destruction and the limitation and regulation of conventional arms. The concept is also closely tied to some fundamental norms found in the Charter—in particular, the duty of States to resolve disputes peacefully and the prohibition of threats or use of force. Even the original GCD proposal put forward in the League of Nations by Maxim Litvinov in 1927 recognized both the need and the right of States to maintain a certain level of armaments for such purposes as maintaining domestic security, defending borders and the maintenance of collective security commitments.[3] The League Covenant did not even address "disarmament" per se; it instead called for "the reduction of national armaments to the lowest point consistent with national safety and the enforcement by common action of international obligations" (article 8). Similar language exists in the United Nations Charter[4] along with additional language concerning the

---

[3] Maxime Litvinoff [original spelling], remarks before the Preparatory Commission for the Disarmament Conference, 30 November 1927, document C.667.M.225.1927 IX (League of Nations: Geneva, 16 January 1928).

[4] Article 26 identified the goal "to promote the establishment and maintenance of international peace and security with the least diversion for armaments of the world's human and economic resources".

supply of armed forces for peacekeeping functions—another indicator that States would be allowed to retain some military capabilities for specific security functions.

In short, neither the Covenant nor the Charter was a pacifist document: both recognized that arms do have a role to play in the maintenance of international peace and security as well as domestic order. It is up to the States to decide which armaments are to be prohibited, which are to be permitted, what shall be the ground rules governing their use, what shall be the size and specific functions of the remaining military forces and other such issues. This is to be accomplished internationally through the process of negotiating multilateral treaties—and, as it has been noted earlier in this volume, some 12 multilateral treaties refer explicitly to GCD as a goal transcending their individual objectives. The fact that the States have not fully implemented the various obligations associated with GCD is hardly due to any flaw in the concept or the goal.

Another line of attack on general and complete disarmament

The pursuit of a comprehensive approach to disarmament commenced shortly after the end of the Second World War and culminated in the United Nations General Assembly's GCD resolution in 1959 and the McCloy-Zorin joint statement of 1961. A great advocate of comprehensive disarmament was Philip Noel-Baker, whose Nobel Peace Prize Lecture in 1959 discussed at length the pros and cons of pursuing disarmament by a comprehensive approach as opposed to relying on "partial measures". How ironic it is that today this same dichotomy is reflected in policy statements by States that possess nuclear weapons. The current term for "partial measures" is the so-called "step-by-step process", which identifies a number of preconditions that must be satisfied before disarmament is possible. In short, these States adopt a sequential approach to disarmament, with steps A, B, C, etc. necessarily occurring before step Z (nuclear disarmament) is achieved.

A list of these preconditions is breathtaking in scope. They have included preventing the proliferation of nuclear weapons and other weapons of mass destruction, resolving all regional disputes, "international stability" based on the "principle of undiminished security for all", preventing nuclear terrorism, achieving détente among the great powers, outlawing space weapons and many others. In short, nuclear disarmament will require nothing less than World Peace—a nirvana on Earth—achieved sequentially through all these various "steps".[5] In this vision, nuclear disarmament has either no role or only a minimal contribution to international peace and security—security becomes in this view a precondition for disarmament. Yet the pursuit of security without disarmament is itself a fantasy, given the insecurities and instabilities produced by arms races, asymmetric arsenals and never-ending qualitative improvements of weaponry. Here it becomes more apparent than ever that, if there is one approach that is more idealistic and utopian than comprehensive GCD, it is the step-by-step process: there will simply never be a global consensus in support of such an approach that is so obviously intended to perpetuate possession.

The defensive parapet of general and complete disarmament

Ironically, the great advantage of GCD approach is not to be found so much in its idealism, but in its realism. The GCD approach recognizes that "security in a world without nuclear weapons" is not a problem to be solved only after nuclear weapons have been abolished. International initiatives driven by GCD fully recognize that nuclear disarmament will not occur or be sustainable in isolation of other considerations

---

[5] It is noteworthy in this respect that the American GCD proposal in 1961 was put forward at the United Nations as an initiative for GCD "in a peaceful world". See United Nations Department of State Publication 7277, "The United States Program for General and Complete Disarmament in a Peaceful World", September 1961.

of international peace and security, including the status of conventional force holdings, the levels of military spending and modernization, controls over the use of force, the availability of arenas and instruments for the peaceful resolution of disputes and international adjudication of disputes. These are all not preconditions for disarmament *to* occur, but measures that are necessary to sustain disarmament *as* it occurs. The fundamental difference here is between the GCD approach of "progress *in* disarmament" and the step-by-step approach of "progress *towards* disarmament". The stronger these agreed measures will be in implementing disarmament commitments, the better will the ability of the disarmament community be to refute chronic claims by weapons advocates that nuclear disarmament would only lead to a new, unstable age of conventional wars.

Over many decades, the multilateral disarmament machinery of the United Nations has generated an international consensus on five standards for quality disarmament arrangements: verification; transparency; irreversibility; bindingness; and universality. To the extent that the international community implements such standards, most of the claims routinely made by the "Dirty Dozen" will lose any semblance of credibility. Together, these norms constitute the "gold standard" not just of disarmament, but for a wider approach to international peace and security. At the very least, the residual risks associated with a GCD arrangement—including the old spectres of "break-out" and cheating—would pale by comparison with the risks that would exist in a world either without disarmament or a world intent on pursuing it only as goal to be achieved after World Peace. This is the very essence of GCD as a security concept: it anticipates future security challenges—such as the role of conventional arms in a post-nuclear-weapon world and the need to significantly strengthen norms and institutions for the peaceful resolution of disputes—and addresses such challenges now, rather than awaiting the advent of nirvana.

Some observations on the future of general and complete disarmament

No one can reliably predict which specific approach to GCD would be the most auspicious to pursue—a single comprehensive treaty would be only one possible option. Others would include a GCD "framework convention" that sets forth principles for future multinational negotiations; perhaps this could begin with a new Russian–United States joint statement updating McCloy-Zorin.[6] It is about time to revisit that statement.

The Conference on Disarmament in Geneva has been unable to negotiate any multilateral treaty in two decades and has specifically not produced any results on the "comprehensive programme of disarmament" on its agenda. The "consensus rule" will likely continue to hinder progress in GCD, as well as in advancing partial measures. Yet if the principle of "universality" is to be taken seriously as a disarmament norm, the simple notion of dispensing with the consensus rule may prove to be both impossible in practice and illogical in theory.

Several actions could help to revive GCD as a focus for future progress in disarmament. The United Nations General Assembly, which routinely cites this term in its resolutions, has done little to place it at the centre of multilateral disarmament efforts, while continuing to cite it as an "ultimate goal". It could implement its responsibilities under Article 11 of the Charter and adopt an annual resolution reaffirming the relevance and importance of GCD as a global priority, while setting forth some principles to guide its implementation. The United Nations currently approaches "disarmament, demilitarization and reintegration" (DDR) strictly as an activity that follows the end of domestic conflicts—why should this concept not also apply to nuclear disarmament? The existence of a credible "defence conversion" capability may well help to neutralize

---

[6] See A/4879.

institutional resistance to disarmament based on fears of plant closures and budget cuts.[7]

The relationship between a "nuclear weapons convention" and GCD requires further study. Advocates of the former rarely if ever discuss this issue and, in some cases, treat nuclear disarmament as an end in itself—a goal to be pursued with little attention to its full implications for international peace and security in a world without such weapons but replete with conventional arms.[8] A comprehensive GCD treaty could conceivably incorporate a ban on nuclear weapons, though negotiating such a treaty would certainly prove to be complex and time-consuming.

United Nations Secretary-General Ban Ki-moon has offered his own approach—his five-point nuclear disarmament proposal of 24 October 2008 called for either a nuclear weapons convention or "agreement on a framework of separate, mutually reinforcing instruments" with the same goal.[9] His proposal, however, was not limited to nuclear disarmament. His fifth point included several "complementary measures" including "the elimination of other types of WMD [weapons of mass destruction]; new efforts against WMD terrorism; limits on the production and trade in conventional arms; and new weapons bans, including of missiles and space weapons". He

---

[7] For an early by rare example of how this issue has been approached by the United Nations, see the study on the economic and social consequences of disarmament, commissioned by ECOSOC and published in 1962 as document E/3593/Rev.1.

[8] The "Model Nuclear Weapons Convention" (General Assembly document A/62/650, 18 January 2008), circulated at the United Nations in 2008, contains one passing reference to GCD in its preamble—as a goal—but does not address the nexus between nuclear disarmament and conventional arms control. Similarly, the current campaign for a "ban the bomb" treaty among like-minded States also fails to address the relationship of nuclear disarmament to other security challenges, while also falling short on the norm of universality.

[9] The full text is available from http://www.un.org/apps/news/infocus/sgspeeches/search_full.asp?statID=351 (accessed 4 August 2016).

clearly viewed nuclear disarmament in its wider context, calling his proposal "a fresh start not just on disarmament, but to strengthen our system of international peace and security."

The scholarly and research community could certainly devote more attention to this issue, having essentially ignored it for decades. They could begin by exploring more closely the relationship between nuclear disarmament and conventional arms control, a subject taken up in the next chapter.

Governments, especially in the nuclear-weapon States, should be encouraged to establish (or re-establish) disarmament agencies that would serve as an internal source of advocacy for disarmament, as a resource to support ongoing diplomatic initiatives and as an institutional means to take on the critics of disarmament. The military and defence sectors of these Governments should be engaged as active participants in the disarmament process, rather than viewed as adversaries to confront. Their cooperation will be vital in achieving real progress in such areas as verification, transparency and irreversibility, as well as in responding credibly to disarmament critics. Reorienting military research and development away from weapons development to the "nuts and bolts" of disarmament as a security policy is perhaps the most urgent task of all, as is the need for the military to take more seriously defence issues not involving weaponry, such as the evolution of a defence strategy focused on human security.

Another constituency that potentially can contribute much to the advancement of nuclear disarmament includes those sectors of Governments (and international organizations) that are seeking to promote social and economic development. While the relationship between disarmament and development has a long history in United Nations deliberations, a stalemate continues between the rich and poor countries over the nature of that relationship, or even whether it exists at all. The scholarly and research community has much to offer in potentially breaking this stalemate by emphasizing the nature of an "opportunity cost"—that is, by highlighting for the development community the enormous scale of resources that are being diverted to nuclear weapons and other military purposes at the expense of meeting basic human development needs, which, if met, will pay their own security dividends.

Living up to the goals set forth by the United Nations Charter

Clearly GCD is about much more than disarmament—it offers an integrated approach to address the larger "problem of war". This point was well recognized even back in 1952 when the United States proposed some principles to serve as a basis for a disarmament programme. "The goal of disarmament", the proposal began, "is not to regulate but to prevent war by relaxing the tensions and fears created by armaments and by making war inherently, as it is constitutionally under the Charter, impossible as a means of settling disputes between nations."[10]

A strong case could be made that GCD, to the extent that it can succeed in eliminating weapons of mass destruction, limiting conventional arms and military spending, promoting the peaceful settlement of disputes and strengthening the norm against the threat or use of force, has the potential to make an enormously positive contribution to international peace and security; this is the GCD multiplier. And in so doing, it also has the potential to liberate vast economic and technological resources for meeting basic human needs, which would produce even more dividends for peace and security. Hence GCD is not a relic of a bygone era. It needs first to be discussed among States. Then it needs to be acted upon. And it is needed now more than ever.

---

[10] "Proposal of the United States: Essential Principles for a Disarmament Programme", United Nations Disarmament Commission, DC/C.1/1, 24 April 1952.

Philip Noel-Baker's Nobel Peace Prize Lecture concluded with the following: "Disarmament is not a policy by itself; it is part of the general policy of the UN. But it is a vital part of that policy; without it, the UN institutions can never function as they should."[11] Indeed, the future of the United Nations as an international organization will be very much dependent upon whether GCD remains merely an "ultimate goal" or whether it actually starts to guide the actions of States, thus giving both peace and prosperity a chance. Without the multiplier, there will only be perpetual division.

---

[11] Philip Noel-Baker, Nobel Peace Prize Lecture, Oslo, 11 December 1959.

Hard and soft linkages between nuclear and conventional disarmament

Paul Meyer
Adjunct Professor and Fellow, Simon Fraser University
Senior Fellow, Simons Foundation
Ambassador (retired), Canadian Foreign Service

Not surprising for an organization forged in the fires and carnage of the Second World War, the United Nations has from the beginning been preoccupied with the issue of disarmament. As noted earlier in this volume, it was the subject of the very first resolution passed by the General Assembly at its first session in 1946. That resolution created an Atomic Energy Commission, which among its tasks was to develop proposals "for the elimination from national armaments of atomic weapons and of all other major weapons adaptable to mass destruction".[1] It has also been noted that, while atomic weapons were singled out in this resolution, its scope was not limited to these and the direction was to eliminate all other weapons capable of mass slaughter. This tasking to abolish the most destructive weapons in national arsenals was situated in broader efforts aimed at the "early general regulation and reduction of armaments and armed forces".[2]

This holistic approach to disarmament did not make the elimination of any weapon system contingent on the elimination of some other system or indeed on any other action. The clear expectation of the General Assembly was that these desired disarmament steps would be forthcoming as part of a general reduction and regulation of armed forces around the globe. Such an approach was in keeping with the provisions of the United Nations Charter. Article 26 of the Charter calls for the maintenance of international peace and security with the least

---

[1] General Assembly resolution 1 (I) of 24 January 1946.
[2] General Assembly resolution 41 of 13 December 1946.

diversion of human and economic resources for armaments. It further tasks the Security Council with developing a plan for the international regulation of armaments. Regrettably, 70 years later we still await this plan from the Council.

The onset of the cold war and the rising mistrust among the erstwhile allies prevented the realization of Article 26 and other Charter provisions for a functional collective security system. The cold war did not, however, exclude cooperation between the rival superpowers when it was judged in their security interests to do so. It was also expedient for this cooperation to be framed as part of efforts to avoid "the devastation that would be visited upon all mankind by a nuclear war ...".[3] Thus, at the instigation of the United States and the Soviet Union, the Treaty on the Non-Proliferation of Nuclear Weapons (NPT) was concluded in 1968 and entered into force in 1970.

The issue of disarmament, in a treaty motivated by the desires of its nuclear weapon–armed sponsors to prevent further spread of this capability to others, was set out in its article VI. In the famous or infamous formulation contained in article VI, all NPT States parties are "to pursue negotiations in good faith on effective measures relating to cessation of the nuclear arms race at an early date and to nuclear disarmament, and on a treaty on general and complete disarmament under strict and effective international control".

What has been problematic about this formulation, beyond the vague direction on nuclear disarmament negotiations, has been the claim by some that a linkage existed between nuclear disarmament and general and complete disarmament to the effect that the former could not be accomplished until the latter was achieved. The suggestion that the treaty on general and complete disarmament envisaged by article VI is somehow a precondition for nuclear disarmament is rejected

---

[3] Preamble of the Treaty on the Non-Proliferation of Nuclear Weapons of 1968.

by many especially among the non-nuclear-weapon States as a mere pretext for delay on the part of the nuclear-weapon States in fulfilling their nuclear disarmament commitment. (See especially the chapter in this volume by John Burroughs, entitled "Legal aspects of general and complete disarmament".)

This opposition has not however persuaded some nuclear-weapon States to cease affirming that linkage in their public statements. Most recently at the 2015 NPT Review Conference (27 April to 22 May) in New York, the representatives of some nuclear-weapon States asserted that a form of linkage existed between progress on nuclear disarmament and the achievement of other security aims associated with general and complete disarmament. In his address to the Review Conference's Main Committee I devoted to disarmament, one such delegation declared, "Approaches which fail to take into account the strategic context will not help us to make progress. The NPT approach is pragmatic: nuclear disarmament, under Article VI, falls in the context of general and complete disarmament. It fully takes into account the strategic context."[4]

Another representative at the Review Conference stressed that "nuclear disarmament should be carried out under conditions of strategic stability and equal security for all". These factors are deteriorating and the existence of "grave imbalances in conventional weapons in the European continent do not facilitate further steps in the nuclear missiles field as well". As an alternative to those advocating a nuclear weapons convention to achieve a "nuclear zero", this delegation suggested that "in accordance with the penultimate paragraph of the Preamble and with Article VI of the Treaty, the total

---

[4] Jean Hugues Simon-Michel, Permanent Representative of France to the Conference of Disarmament, statement to the NPT Review Conference, Main Committee I, "Nuclear Disarmament and security assurances", Geneva, 1 May 2015.

elimination of nuclear arsenals should take place in compliance with the Treaty on General and Complete Disarmament."[5]

These reaffirmations of linkage between achieving nuclear disarmament and the conclusion of a treaty on general and complete disarmament is a reminder that some leading nuclear powers still wish to combine the two goals of article VI as if the strategic comma separating them did not exist. The vast majority of States will continue to reject any hard linkage between nuclear disarmament and general and complete disarmament. In doing so, they will be standing on solid ground in terms of agreed United Nations policy. Notably at its first special session devoted to disarmament (SSOD-I) held in 1978, the General Assembly specified priority measures on disarmament. While noting that "the ultimate objective of the efforts of states in the disarmament process is general and complete disarmament under effective international control", the General Assembly also stipulated that, among such measures of disarmament, "effective measures of nuclear disarmament and the prevention of nuclear war have the highest priority".[6] Accordingly, effective measures of nuclear disarmament should be implemented on a priority basis, irrespective of progress towards the wider goal of general and complete disarmament.

If States (and concerned civil society) are correct to reject "hard linkage" as a pretext for delaying movement on nuclear disarmament, they should be open to acknowledging a "soft linkage" between these two multilaterally sanctioned goals. The security reality is that the world is awash in conventional arms from small arms to major weapon systems. Despite long-standing policy direction, including from the United

---

[5] Mikhail I. Uliyanov, Acting Head of the delegation of the Russian Federation, statement to the NPT Review Conference, Main Committee I, 1 May 2015.

[6] Final Document of the tenth special session of the General Assembly, S-10/2, 30 June 1978, paras. 19 and 20.

Nations Charter, stipulating that States should reduce these arms to the minimal levels required for self-defence, action on conventional disarmament has been limited.

In fact little has been done at the universal level to control armaments and, compared to its detailed guidance on weapons of mass destruction disarmament, the outcome of SSOD-I offered little direction on conventional disarmament beyond affirming that the "gradual reduction of armed forces and conventional weapons should be resolutely pursued within the framework of progress towards general and complete disarmament".[7]

It has been at the regional level that the most extensive conventional arms control and disarmament agreements have been achieved. It was essentially only in Europe, the focus of the cold war military confrontation, that major arms control and disarmament accords have been negotiated. The Treaty on Conventional Armed Forces in Europe (CFE Treaty) of 1990 led to massive reductions in the level of combat systems. This treaty was complemented by the confidence and security-building measures of the Vienna Document and the cooperative overflight provisions of the Treaty on Open Skies. Unfortunately, an abandonment of efforts to ratify an adapted CFE Treaty has resulted in a 2007 decision by the Russian Federation to suspend its implementation of the Treaty, which in turn has prompted a United States decision to do the same. The revival of East-West tensions in the wake of the Ukrainian crisis has exacerbated the existing problems. There is a real risk that continued neglect of the existing arms control and disarmament regime could lead to a major breakdown of the past achievements and a return to an anarchic security situation in Europe.

It is not in the interest of the international community to ignore the concerns voiced by countries like the Russian

---

[7] Ibid., para. 81.

Federation and China that some developments in the conventional field, such as ballistic missile defences, prompt global strike weapons and the lack of agreed constraints on the placement of conventional weapons in outer space threaten their security and impede further progress on nuclear arms reductions. These concerns deserve some cooperative security responses, be they via further arms control agreements or political arrangements such as confidence-building measures.

Similarly, it is timely to put a spotlight again on the challenge of conventional disarmament in a world where active conflict is not being limited to the proverbial AK-47s and RPGs, but is also involving major combat systems from main battle tanks to self-propelled heavy artillery in countries such as the Syrian Arab Republic, Iraq, Libya, Sudan and eastern Ukraine. If it requires a bloody conflict to galvanize action, the current situation should motivate States and civil society actors alike to return their attention to the threats posed by conventional arms. There is a pressing need to re-engage diplomatic processes to reinforce existing agreements in Europe and to develop new arrangements to extend the reach of conventional arms control to other regions. It is in this way that we can best pay homage to the goal of general and complete disarmament through relevant, concrete action.

General and complete disarmament and defence policies

Alyson J. K. Bailes
Adjunct Professor, University of Iceland
Director (retired), Stockholm International Peace Research Institute
Ambassador (retired), British Diplomatic Service

It may seem strange to expect defence ministries and military alliances to care about reducing arms on the path to total disarmament, but there are at least two good reasons why they should. First are their own stated aims; it would be a rare defence ministry these days that defined its mission as to make war and destroy things. More typically, these institutions claim that their military activities are designed to preserve the peace and they commit themselves to act within the framework of international law, including United Nations principles. Logically, then, they should respect the United Nations goal of general and complete disarmament (GCD) in no less than Article 51 of the United Nations Charter, which validates self-defence. Secondly and more practically, to start getting rid of weapons, you need people who understand weapons and can destroy them safely. This is obvious in cases like chemical weapons disposal, but it can also be surprisingly hard and expensive to dismantle a tank or even destroy rifles.

What happens in practice? Despite the lip service, in organizational terms, defence ministries tend to see it as other people's job to worry about cutting arms—typically, it is foreign ministries that house the arms control and disarmament departments—while they focus on amassing as many as they can. Successful defence ministries worldwide pull resources into the armaments business in a double way: by spending soaring amounts on buying arms, and by pressing their Governments to subsidize the weapons industry. A military alliance might support this by urging its members to spend a minimum percentage of their GDP on defence and by praising those who devote a high proportion of this spending to equipment and research and development rather than personnel costs. A general aggravating factor is the typically poor financial control of defence contracts, regularly leading to cost overruns and not infrequently sliding into corruption.

Nor is it just military organizations that boost the defence business. The European Union, for example, stands for peace generally, supports peace missions, proclaims a restrictive code for arms exports and helps to finance many United Nations and other disarmament initiatives. Yet the European Commission and European Defence Agency devote great effort to encouraging the European arms industry to improve its output and global competitiveness through closer integration, freer competition within Europe, more centrally funded research and development and so on. They also run high-cost programmes to boost the development of "security" technologies, which may not involve weapons as such but might be used to make weapons more deadly.

Such policies, and the strivings of related interest groups, are hardly new, but various historical trends have unfortunately helped them to tip the odds against any real progress in GCD. At first after the end of the cold war, massive cuts were achieved in weaponry, thanks to free national decisions— notably, the slashing of German and Russian force levels—as much as to the disarmament deals of the time. In many regions, however, including the Western Balkans within Europe, the loosening of the old bipolar system merely allowed local rivalries to flourish and to spark local arms races. Before long, too, the demands first of the post-9/11 "war on terrorism" and then of the resurfacing of tensions within Europe were driving all European States to restock their defence budgets, scale up their weaponry plans and look for new technological edges to balance their inescapable weaknesses of scale.

Trends at the higher level of policy and philosophy are part of the problem. In the cold war days, the imminent threat of nuclear destruction made nations wary of their own, as well as their adversaries', weapons. Lower levels of arms made sense as a way both to reduce risks of accidentally sparking war and of limiting the destructiveness of war if it came. Nations often talked of seeking "sufficiency" or "minimum" levels in their defence planning. From 1990, however, as fears of retaliation and escalation waned, no one seemed to see a problem in calling for new sophisticated capacities to carry out crisis management missions—long-distance deployments that forced many smaller States to upgrade their hardware and replace conscripts with professional armies. After the shock attacks of 2001, the previous United States Government disregarded legal constraints, including arms limitations, in fighting global terrorism. The interventions in Afghanistan and Iraq, now widely viewed as strategic failures, pushed defence spending back to cold war levels and were a godsend for the whole arms business, including private military companies (on which more is discussed later).

Philosophically, the trouble in arming yourself against something as vague and limitless as terrorism is that there can be no thought of "balance" or negotiating a lower level of confrontation. You have the moral right to bear whatever arms you think necessary and the other side does not. The new stress after 2001 on non-proliferation of weapons of mass destruction similarly distracted attention from the dangers of the "acknowledged" nuclear States' massive arsenals, asserting instead their right to stop anyone else from sharing what they already enjoyed. That attitude all too easily spread, and is still spreading, to the idea of an entitlement to develop superior conventional arms and new destructive technologies, for those who already have most of them. There could hardly be any attitude more likely to spur proliferation of all kinds and more directly contrary to the vision of GCD.

As one among many symptoms of how disarmament has lost its centrality in the new security thinking, the North Atlantic Treaty Organization (NATO) Summit declaration of March 1988 devoted 7 of its 19 paragraphs to arms control and non-proliferation. In the 2010 NATO Strategic Concept, the count is 3 of 38 paragraphs and, in the Wales Summit declaration of September 2014, just 9 of 113 paragraphs.

What can be done? Separating the idea of "defence = national protection" from that of bearing arms is a logical start. There are at least 20 countries in the world without armed forces, and there must be many others for whom the chief risks today are non-military ones. Money saved on weapons need not always go to "soft" causes but could be used to defend against natural disasters, pandemics and cyberattacks, for instance. Organizationally, strong arms control and disarmament departments should be implanted within defence ministries. Everyone involved in defence planning should be required to reflect not just on minimizing lethal equipment but on making it more environment-friendly, less resource-costly and easier to destroy safely. Members of military forces should be routinely trained not only in avoiding forbidden "inhumane" weapons and techniques, but also in the principle of GCD and what may be done at the everyday level to move towards it.

Some less obvious current trends also need tackling. The loss of an "arms control reflex" since the cold war's end has hampered and delayed us in seeing the risks of new (potentially) destructive technologies. It was totally predictable that drones, if allowed to develop freely, would be misused both by untrustworthy Governments and by non-state actors, including terrorists. Finding a disarmament solution to put this genie back in the bottle has become almost impossible as a result. How many more times will we make the same mistake, as other techniques like nanotechnology, robotics, virtual reality and gene manipulation are developed past the weaponization threshold?

Next, defence ministries are being increasingly forced by resource pressure to outsource more supplies and functions from civilians and/or from private business. Is this good or bad for GCD? It may formally reduce military establishments, but the civilians involved are still supporting armed defence and perhaps prolonging its viability. If some military jobs, like guarding premises or search and rescue, could be permanently transferred to unarmed civilians, that would be a more hopeful step. But the opposite has too often happened recently, for instance in Iraq, when private companies took over tasks involving the use of arms—a dangerous trend indeed, as it involves more actors in the weapons game in settings often lacking any proper discipline or legal constraint. How to control illegal non-state weapons flows is already a huge headache for the international community and a challenge to the original idea of GCD as a pact among Governments. It gets worse every time someone pleads for the freedom to sell weapons to "our friends" in some civil war or tussle for power, forgetting all the cases when such weapons have shortly been turned back against "us".

In ending such new-style conflicts and trying to build peace, it has become routine for international organizations to offer programmes of disarmament, demobilization and reintegration for the defeated and/or surplus fighting forces. When well done, including in weapons collection, these also reflect the spirit of GCD. The recognized central government is then, however, encouraged to carry out a broader security sector reform (SSR), re-establishing one legitimate and effective central army, police force and so on. The standard directives of SSR are high-minded, but they are strangely silent on weapons issues and sketchy on defence resource management in general. Surely, the moment of restarting after a conflict or regime change is the ideal time to think about minimizing weaponry, ensuring clean procurement of whatever has to be bought, introducing strict (re-)export controls, joining and faithfully observing all available arms control agreements and so forth. The case of the Western Balkans (Florence Agreement) shows how a timely initiative may allow a whole regional neighbourhood to cut weapons and abide by lower ceilings. More radically, with due international protection, could not some "saved" nations even consider moving to a non-military defence?

Sustainable Development Goals: The need for peacebuilding and measures of disarmament

Richard Jolly
Honorary Professor and Research Associate, Institute of
Development Studies, University of Sussex
Former Special Adviser, United Nations Development Programme
Former Deputy Executive Director, United Nations Children's Fund

"The future we want", the outcome document of the General Assembly open working group on the post-2015 Sustainable Development Goals (SDGs),[1] sets out as Goal 16 the promotion of "peaceful and inclusive societies for sustainable development …". Desirable as this is, it unfortunately is the closest the proposals get to any reference to diminishing national or international conflict, let alone to reducing military expenditures or to measures of disarmament. And this is in spite of the latest United Nations report on the Millennium Development Goals (MDGs), stating that "conflicts remain the biggest threat to human development, with fragile and conflict-affected countries typically experiencing the highest poverty rates".[2] Moreover, the largest failures to achieve rapid progress towards the MDGs have been in countries beset by conflict.

Actions towards promoting peaceful and inclusive societies in Goal 16 are elaborated with either a highly generalized domestic focus (for instance "significantly [to] reduce all forms of violence and related death rates everywhere") or, when made more international, related to legal or institutional advance (for instance promoting "the rule of law at the national and international levels" or broadening and strengthening "the participation of developing countries in the institutions of global

---

[1] A/68/970.
[2] United Nations, "The Millennium Development Goals Report 2015", press release DPI/2594E, New York, 6 July 2015.

governance"). Even the one time-bound specific of Goal 16 (by 2030 significantly to reduce illicit financial and arms flows, strengthen recovery and return of stolen assets and combating all forms of organized crime) clearly relates to criminal activity of theft rather than to civil war or international conflict.

My purpose is not to criticize the SDGs or the process building up to them. The SDGs, in my view, represent a major step forward internationally, an advance on the MDGs and a major step beyond anything that has gone before. The SDGs are, for instance, incomparably more people-focused and less narrowly economistic than the early goals of the first Development Decade put forward by President John F. Kennedy in 1961, which concentrated on an acceleration of economic growth in developing countries. They are certainly more substantive than the MDGs, which emerged (with some further negotiation) from the Millennium Summit of 2000. Moreover, in two respects the proposed SDGs represent a giant step forward internationally: first, because they are universal and apply to all countries and, second, because they are explicitly recognized to require some adaptation by each country to its specific context. Though some commentators have raised doubts about these two new elements, a better reaction in my view is that they strengthen the goals as a *global process* and add *greater realism* to their implementation and monitoring.

But what about the neglect in "The future we want" of actions to diminish conflict, reduce military expenditures and establish new initiatives leading to measures of disarmament? At this late stage, these vital issues must now largely be pursued in parallel rather than formally incorporated as part of the goals. This certainly does not mean that they should be forgotten or seen as irrelevant or unimportant in relation to necessary actions towards the goals. Any actions—national, regional or international—that help reduce conflict will contribute to creating a context within which progress towards the goals can be accelerated. Reductions of conflict will open opportunities for action freed from the destructive and all-distracting preoccupations of war and fighting and especially from the misery and human setbacks they involve for millions of people. Conflict reduction and prevention will also help diminish, though not eliminate, the national and international pressures responsible for millions of people being displaced within their own countries or fleeing as migrants across borders to others. Measures of disarmament can also free up resources for more productive purposes and for the support of actions towards the goals, including indirect actions by creating more stable and sustainable societies.

The United Nations has set forth and supported many actions towards control of conflict and pursuit of peace, in addition to supporting humanitarian services and relief when conflict occurs. Approaches to preventive diplomacy and conflict prevention are important for maintaining the peaceful and inclusive societies in which goals towards the world we want can best be pursued. But where conflict and civil disturbance already exist, strategies of peacemaking and peacebuilding will be needed, and again the United Nations has much practical experience in pursuing them. Such actions to maintain peaceful societies or move towards them will almost always require regional or international actions of support, politically, financially and in other ways.

In today's world of ever greater interconnectedness, broader areas of regional and international action will also be needed if the SDGs are to be achieved. Measures of efficient and effective regional and global governance will therefore need to be strengthened as a matter of priority, as recognized in Goal 16 but over a broader area. Global initiatives will be needed to support positive advance but also to prevent setbacks by tackling such threats as those from climate chaos, famine and agriculture instabilities and cross-border health pandemics. Surges in migration and human trafficking also need regional and global action on a scale far beyond what is envisaged at present. Migration is partly a consequence of conflict and human rights abuses and partly of growing inequalities in a world of rising ambitions and global awareness. And there are more specific economic threats that need stronger measures of global governance—financial instabilities, capital flight and cross-border tax avoidance, international trade competition, and pressures on wages and social welfare in a race to the bottom, among many others. Drives to geopolitical dominance and pressures to build military supremacy are both a consequence and often a cause of these forces and imbalances.

Although history leaves no doubt about the human and economic costs of war and military investment in weapons, efforts to control them and to pursue disarmament with a view to channelling a substantial fraction of the money saved into development of poorer countries are, by comparison, fewer and more limited.

It is true that, in the United Nations, many countries have actually proposed major reductions in military spending. The first such proposal was by the Government of France in 1955,[3] which put forward the idea that the resources released would be paid into a common fund, with a quarter going to development of poorer countries and the rest left for disposal of the country contributing. Variants of such a "disarmament for development" proposal have been made in almost every decade of the United Nations since that time. In 1957, it was put forward by the Soviet Union and, in 1964, by Brazil, which put the focus on using the fund to finance conversion within the arms industry and for economic development. In 1973, the United Nations General Assembly adopted a resolution calling for a 10-per-cent one-time reduction by the five permanent members of the Security Council, with other countries encouraged to join in. In 1978, at the first special session of the General Assembly devoted to disarmament, further proposals were put forward—by Senegal, again by France and

---

[3] *Official Records of the Disarmament Commission, Supplement for April to December 1955*, document DC/71, annex 16.

by Romania. In the 1980s, there were two subsequent special sessions of the General Assembly devoted to disarmament, each with proposals for some measure of disarmament with a part directed to development.[4] The latest substantial United Nations reports on disarmament and development of 1988 (A/43/368) and 2004 (A/59/119) analysed the positive linkages between disarmament and development and identified many policies that could open the way for increasing the benefits from disarmament in the future. In pursuing Goal 16 of the SDGs, countries and United Nations agencies can learn much from a review of these reports and proposals.

But this may not be the real obstacle. The fact is that, despite all the brainwork that went into these United Nations reports and proposals and the sound advice United Nations and governmental experts came up with, none of these grand designs ever materialized. Leaders and policymakers in most countries begin with the feeling that disarmament is a wonderful ideal but one that is not practical for them at the present time. For this reason, and perhaps for this reason alone, practical actions towards disarmament are not taken seriously. This is a great error of thinking! For there are examples and indeed history shows many times that military spending has been reduced—which have subsequently led to positive economic consequences.

Between the late 1980s and late 1990s, major reductions in worldwide military expenditures occurred, in line with those called for in the 1988 report (A/43/368). These emerged from ending the cold war and the fundamental political and economic changes that followed, beyond anything envisaged only a few years earlier. World military expenditure decreased by a third

---

[4] A summary of these resolutions can be found in Richard Jolly et al, *UN Contributions to Development Thinking and Practice* (Bloomington, Indiana University Press), 2004, p. 241.

(in constant prices) over the decade from 1988 to 1998.[5] In North America, it was reduced by 31 per cent and in Western Europe by about half of this. In the Russian Federation and East and Central Europe, the decline was very much greater. In fact, every region of the world reduced military expenditures over this period, except the Middle East. Although there was no peace dividend in the sense that resources saved from the military were directly and specifically channelled into national and international development, disarmament gave a strong and sustained boost to economic growth and the 1990s became a period of international growth and dynamism.

Less emphasized have been the practical actions towards disarmament taken by individual countries, Costa Rica and Panama most notably, to abolish their armies and run their countries without military forces. Indeed, more than 20 countries exist today without an army and are often highly successful economically and politically in following this route.

Changes in military spending since the new millennium have been more mixed and much less positive. In 1998 the arms race began again. This time, it was not even clear who the race was against! But increases in military expenditures in North America, Europe and Asia have moved into high gear. Military spending also started rising again rapidly in Africa and the Middle East to levels that are now about two and a half times greater than their levels in 1987. In East and Central Europe, military spending fell precipitately over the 1990s with the collapse of the Soviet Union but since then has risen rapidly, although so far to levels less than a third of 1987 levels. In Western Europe, military spending first fell over the 1990s, then rose continuously until 2010, but has since been reduced as cutbacks from austerity have taken hold.

---

[5] All data on military spending are taken from the SIPRI Military Expenditure Database. Available from www.sipri.org (accessed 1 March 2016).

World military spending at the time of writing was about 2.3 per cent of gross domestic product, compared to 5.4 per cent in 1988. About three quarters of the developing countries for which data was available in 2011 reduced their military spending over the 1990s and did not increase it subsequently. This means that at least 40 developing countries have maintained a reduced level of spending since the end of the cold war. Though international negotiations leading to comprehensive treaties are an ideal, the above experiences show that partial steps of arms control and reduction in military expenditures are both possible and at times politically more realistic than global agreements. Notwithstanding, regional and global action can often help. For instance, as part of ending civil war and conflict, support for the demobilization of soldiers and their immediate employment in alternative occupations is of critical importance. Without this, they may continue fighting or keep their weapons and move into criminal activities of theft. In the case of child soldiers, alternatives might involve further education or training, although this needs to be skilfully planned if young people are to be creatively engaged after the challenges and excitement of their previous lives. Support for such actions may be regional, as in East Asia with the ending of the Viet Nam war and the regional measures adopted after the financial crisis of 1998-2000, which established regional institutions and agreements to avoid repetition.

In conclusion, although Goal 16 of the SDGs lacks many specifics to guide action, there is a wealth of regional and country experience to show what can be done, which demonstrates the positive economic and social impact that can follow. Promoting peaceful and inclusive societies for sustainable development remains a key objective in its own right and often a critical means towards the achievement of the other SDGs.

A circle that can't be squared: Broad-spectrum arms racing and nuclear disarmament

Jacqueline Cabasso
Executive Director, Western States Legal Foundation

Andrew Lichterman
Senior Research Analyst, Western States Legal Foundation

A Möbius band is a surface with only one side and only one boundary. It can be made with a strip of twisted paper and tape. As described by Wikipedia, "If an ant were to crawl along the length of this strip, it would return to its starting point having traversed the entire length of the strip (on both sides of the original paper) without ever crossing an edge."

Imagine a Möbius strip: one side represents nuclear disarmament and the other general and complete disarmament (GCD). The ant's journey is analogous to the United Nations' 70-year pursuit of nuclear disarmament and GCD.

There is an inextricable relationship between nuclear disarmament and GCD. This paper addresses two aspects: "strategic stability" with the introduction of high-tech non-nuclear weapons that could be used to attack nuclear and other strategically important military systems; and the ways in which continued arms racing and high levels of arms spending undermine human security.

Strategic stability

Over the past 25 years, wars and confrontations between major and regional powers have led to the continuation and modernization of strategically significant weapons systems that originated in the cold war. The purported—and often exaggerated—threat of acquisition of nuclear, chemical or biological weapons both served as a stalking horse for other geopolitical agendas and as a rationale to keep high-tech weapons programmes alive. The best-known examples of this have been the continued development and deployment of ballistic missile defences and programmes to develop "prompt global strike" systems. There are significant technical obstacles to developing practical non-nuclear weapons for prompt global strike. But many of the technologies being researched, such as advances in guidance systems and hypersonic flight, could be applied to the next generation of nuclear delivery systems as well.

Perhaps even more alarming has been the general advance of powerful, long-range and precise conventional weapons and stealthy delivery platforms, together with advances in surveillance, coordination and targeting, because they are more numerous and already deployed and tested in warfare. During the post–cold war period, one country has been both the technology leader in advanced weapons development and by far the largest military spender. Security analysts have been raising concerns for years that conventional "alternatives" to nuclear weapons might pose an obstacle to nuclear arms control negotiations. In 2009, Alexei Arbatov at the Carnegie Moscow Center observed, for example, that "there are very few countries in the world that are afraid of American nuclear weapons. But there are many countries which are afraid of American conventional weapons. In particular, nuclear weapons states like China and Russia are primarily concerned about growing American conventional, precision-guided, long-range capability". He added that "threshold states" with the potential for developing nuclear weapons are similarly concerned about United States conventional capabilities.

Illustrating the salience of advanced conventional weaponry in a post–cold war world, Robert Einhorn, a Special Advisor for non-proliferation and arms control to Secretary of State Hillary Clinton, remarked in 2007, "We should be putting far more effort into developing more effective conventional weapons. It's hard to imagine a president using nuclear weapons under almost any circumstance, but no one doubts our willingness to use conventional weapons."

As antagonisms among the leading nuclear-armed States have slowly ramped up, other States have moved to catch up with the leading military power in some areas (such as hypersonic vehicle efforts) and to counter it in others. One result, but not the only one, has been the slow resumption of nuclear arms racing, in the form of nuclear weapons "modernization" programmes pursued by all nuclear-armed States. Nuclear arms competition seems likely to intensify. The renewed confrontation sparked by the Ukraine crisis added impetus to existing plans to modernize the world's largest nuclear arsenals. The resumption of nuclear competition among the most powerful militaries threatens to stop disarmament progress altogether. Meanwhile, the other nuclear powers continue to expand their arsenals, intensifying the danger of nuclear war in potential flashpoints from the Middle East to South Asia to the Western Pacific.

The danger today is that the new technologies that have been developed in years of continuous "small" wars will combine with nuclear arsenals, still of civilization-destroying size, that have come down to us from the cold war. Stealthy, precision-stand-off weapons and delivery platforms face sophisticated air defences and increasingly capable missile defences. Both offence and defence use electronic warfare measures and now cyberwarfare to jam sensor systems and target the weaknesses of computer-dependent systems. With the increased dependence of militaries on satellites for a wide range of military functions, we can also expect intensified military competition in space.

The speed and complexity of the interactions of all these technologies and the immense volumes of data involved accelerate the trend towards automating elements of decision-making, even where human beings remain formally in the loop. This has been a problem since the depths of the cold war, but it is a problem that has continued to grow. These systems contribute to new imponderables in confrontations between countries that also have nuclear arms. And it is escalation of this kind of warfare that, should it get out of hand, would lead to nuclear war. All this increases the danger of miscalculation in a crisis, amid a global context that is generating crises involving nuclear-armed countries at an accelerating pace.

The development of more sophisticated conventional military capabilities by the most technologically advanced nuclear-armed countries is unlikely to be compatible with progress towards nuclear disarmament. How will potential nuclear adversaries with fewer economic resources respond? Won't they have an incentive to maintain or acquire nuclear weapons to counter the conventional military superiority of potential adversaries? And won't that, in turn, entrench the determination of their more powerful rivals to retain and modernize their own nuclear arsenals, rendering the goal of nuclear disarmament nearly impossible? This conundrum poses one of the biggest challenges to the elimination of nuclear weapons.

The current round of arms racing is being shaped but not impeded by negotiations and treaties on nuclear arms reductions. The cold war and post–cold war approach to disarmament was quantitative, based mainly on bringing down the insanely huge cold war nuclear stockpile numbers, presumably en route to zero. Now, disarmament has been turned on its head. While pruning away the grotesque cold war excesses, what nuclear-armed States portray as nuclear disarmament progress has come to mean "fewer but newer" weapons, with an emphasis on huge long-term investments in nuclear weapons infrastructure, qualitative improvements in the weapons themselves projected for decades to come and new programmes to develop high-tech non-nuclear weapon systems. Nuclear arsenals of civilization-destroying size remain, while a virtually uncontrolled "conventional" arms race of growing complexity places new roadblocks on the path to nuclear disarmament.

The dynamics surrounding ratification of the New START (Strategic Arms Reduction Treaty) Treaty of 2010 are a case in point. The resolution of ratification adopted by the United States Senate included commitments to massive investments in the nuclear weapons infrastructure and modernization programme and to continued development of national missile defences. The Senate also successfully obtained assurances that the Treaty places no limits on the development and deployment of new kinds of non-nuclear missiles and delivery vehicles with non-ballistic trajectories, such as the boost-glide concepts being explored for prompt global strike.[1]

The conditions attached to the Senate ratification in the United States significantly compromised the value of the Treaty as a disarmament measure. Senator Bob Corker from Tennessee, home to the Oak Ridge National Laboratory (site of a proposed multi-billion dollar uranium processing facility), emphasized the compatibility of the New START Treaty with long-term possession of a large nuclear arsenal and continued development of missile defences:

> I ... am proud that as a result of ratification we have been successful in securing commitments from the administration on modernization of our nuclear arsenal and support of our missile defense programs, two things that would not have happened otherwise. In fact, thanks in part to the contributions my staff and I have been able to make, *the new START treaty could easily be called the "Nuclear Modernization and Missile Defense Act of 2010.* [emphasis added]

Final ratification of the New START Treaty by the Russian Duma was subject to its own reciprocal conditions, including the Russian President's obligation to undertake a programme to modernize the Russian Federation's strategic nuclear forces. Grounds for the Russian Federation's withdrawal include the

---

[1] United States Department of State, Bureau of Arms Control, Verification and Compliance, Fact Sheet, "Investments in Conventional Prompt Global Strike", 13 December 2010.

unilateral deployment by the United States of missile defence systems and the adoption of strategic non-nuclear (prompt global strike) weapon systems by the United States without the Russian Federation's approval.

The conditions stipulated by the Duma reflected the 2010 Russian Military Doctrine, which retained a first-use option and reserved the right to use nuclear weapons not only in response to a nuclear attack or an attack with biological or chemical weapons, but also in response to a conventional attack. It also identified the deployment of strategic missile defence systems, the militarization of outer space and the deployment of precision non-nuclear strategic weapon systems as threats that undermine global security. In 2010, the doctrine also introduced, for the first time, the use of high-precision conventional weapons to provide for strategic deterrence, along with nuclear weapons.

A growing number of countries are now working to develop hypersonic weapons for long-range non-nuclear strike systems as part of efforts to defeat missile defences, which up to now have not been designed to counter them. While ballistic missiles follow predictable trajectories in the vacuum of space, hypersonic missiles, flying within the atmosphere, can manoeuvre and change course unpredictably, are less visible to early-warning radars and could only be intercepted by endoatmospheric defences. It should be noted that technologies putatively developed for new kinds of non-nuclear weapons with global reach could also be used to upgrade nuclear-weapon delivery systems.

The development of advanced new non-nuclear strategic weapons is increasingly at odds with the stated objective of nuclear disarmament. As recognized by Russian Foreign Minister Sergei Lavrov in 2010, "to move toward a nuclear-free world, it is necessary to resolve the question of non-nuclear-equipped strategic offensive weapons and strategic weapons in general ...".

Former Soviet President Mikhail Gorbachev saw this coming. At a high-level conference in Rome in 2009 he warned that the pursuit of "military superiority would be an insurmountable obstacle to ridding the world of nuclear weapons. *Unless we discuss demilitarization of international politics, the reduction of military budgets, preventing militarization of outer space, talking about a nuclear-free world will be just rhetorical.*" [emphasis added]

In addition to the threat of catastrophic war directly posed by the resumption of arms racing among the nuclear powers, military-industrial complexes and great power foreign policies that give a central role to the military force continue to be a primary driver of war. Nuclear-armed States account for three quarters of global arms exports; the top two exporting States together account for over half.[2] Imported arms turn local, low-intensity conflicts into industrial-scale wars that fragment societies, destroy vital infrastructure and destabilize entire regions. These human catastrophes are used to justify competing armed interventions that raise the stakes even higher, with nuclear-armed militaries operating in close quarters in proxy confrontations that could easily spiral out of control. A small fraction of humanity benefits in the short run from these high stakes competitions; yet all of us bear the risk.

Redefining security

In 1994, Dr. Mahbub Ul Haq, head of the United Nations Development Programme addressed the question, "What happened to the peace dividend?" in a public forum held at the United Nations. Dr. Ul Haq spoke eloquently of the need for a fundamental transformation in the concept of security, which he described as "the security of people, not just of territory;

---

[2] Pieter D. Wezeman and Siemon T. Wezeman, "Trends in International Arms Transfers, 2014", SIPRI Fact Sheet, Stockholm International Peace Research Institute, March 2015 (Table 1: The 10 largest exporters of major weapons and their main clients, 2010–14).

the security of individuals, not just of nations; security through development, not through arms; security of all the people everywhere—in their homes, in their jobs, in their streets, in their communities and in their environment". This new interpretation, he explained, requires us to regard human security as "universal, global and indivisible".

Article 26 of the United Nations Charter states,

In order to promote the establishment and maintenance of international peace and security with the least diversion for armaments of the world's human and economic resources, the Security Council shall be responsible for formulating ... plans to be submitted to the Members of the United Nations for the establishment of a system for the regulation of armaments. [emphasis added]

Unfortunately, this commitment has not been implemented. In general, the United Nations has failed to link its disarmament and development goals, the original nuclear disarmament and GCD goals, with the Millennium Development Goals, now the Sustainable Development Goals.

Historically, some leaders have recognized the requirements for real security. In his visionary 1941 State of the Union address, before the United States entered the Second World War, President Franklin Roosevelt declared:

In the future days, which we seek to make secure, we look forward to a world founded upon four essential human freedoms.

The first is freedom of speech and expression—everywhere in the world.

The second is freedom of every person to worship God in his own way—everywhere in the world.

The third is freedom from want—which, translated into world terms, means economic understandings which will secure to every nation a healthy peacetime life for its inhabitants—everywhere in the world.

The fourth is freedom from fear—which, translated into world terms, means a world-wide reduction of armaments to such a point and in such a thorough fashion that no nation will be in a position to commit an act of physical aggression against any neighbor—anywhere in the world.

Significantly, he did not consider this to be a utopian goal. According to Roosevelt, "That is no vision of a distant millennium. It is a definite basis for a kind or world attainable in our own time and generation." Foreign and domestic policies premised on the perpetual accumulation of arms and an open-ended war on terror call into question all of those freedoms.

Kirk Boyd of the International Bill of Rights Association expressed it well when he advocated against the promotion of ideologies based on "the false impression ... that there is greater security in weapons and the military than in freedom from want. The truth is we will never reach the fourth freedom, freedom from fear, if we rely on the military alone".[3]

General and complete disarmament as a unifying framework

In recent years there has been a proliferation of single-issue humanitarian disarmament campaigns. These include the following: Control Arms Coalition (arms trade); International Action Network on Small Arms; Campaign to Stop Killer Robots; Cluster Munition Coalition; International Campaign to Abolish Nuclear Weapons; International Campaign to Ban Landmines; International Network on Explosive Weapons;

---

[3] J. Kirk Boyd, "Path to a world free from want and fear", *San Francisco Chronicle*, 12 February 2004.

Toxic Remnants of War Network (dealing with environmental impacts of war); and groups working to ban drones, incendiary weapons, cyberweapons and the weaponization of outer space.

These campaigns share a welcome common focus on humanitarian impacts, but they don't necessarily share a common focus on general disarmament. There is a danger that focusing solely on one weapon system could imply support for or acceptance of another. This calls to mind an arcade game, "whack a mole", in which players use a mallet to try and hit randomly appearing toy moles back into their holes, as other moles pop up. Participants in disarmament discourse sometimes seem to lose track of the basic precept that the purpose of their work is not to regulate how people are killed, but to stop the killing. It is worth remembering that this also was the central purpose of the United Nations Charter, the treaty with the most signatories of all.

In fact, nearly all of the single-weapon issues and the relationship between disarmament and development were listed in the First Committee allocation of agenda items under general and complete disarmament of 18 September 2015.[4]

GCD could be used as an overarching context for the single-issue campaigns and as a framework for mobilizing international public opinion. The difficulties posed by any programme of general disarmament by the current climate of renewed confrontation among the world's most powerful States also could sharpen focus on addressing the causes of armed conflict as a necessary element of any practical disarmament programme.

Conclusion

The concept of security should be reframed at every level of society and government, with a premium on universal human, economic and ecological security, a return to

---

[4] A/C.1/70/1, annex (item 11).

multilateralism, and a commitment to cooperative, non-violent means of conflict resolution. Nuclear disarmament should serve as the leading edge of a global trend towards GCD and redirection of military expenditures to meet human needs and protect the environment.

Progress towards a global society that is more fair, peaceful and ecologically sustainable is interdependent. We are unlikely to get far on any of these objectives without progress on all. They are not "preconditions" for disarmament but, together with disarmament, are preconditions for human survival. In our relationships both with each other and the planet, we are now hard up against the choice Dr. Martin Luther King, Jr., warned about: non-violence or non-existence.

Part 3
The way forward

Upholding the United Nations Charter and general and complete disarmament: The Costa Rican perspective

Maritza Chan
Former Minister Counsellor
Permanent Mission of Costa Rica to the United Nations

In 1945, "we the peoples" of the United Nations pledged "to save succeeding generations from the scourge of war, which twice in our lifetime has brought untold sorrow to mankind".[1] Integral to this commitment was the premise that disarmament, including the elimination of all weapons of mass destruction and the regulation and reduction of armaments and armed forces, was a necessary step towards achieving the ambitious international peace and security goals of the United Nations. This article critically examines the statutory basis, as well as the past, present and future roles, of the primary United Nations institutions responsible for disarmament—namely, the General Assembly and the Security Council. Finally, it considers how they can be better utilized in the name of this ambitious goal and in fulfilment of the United Nations Charter.

In keeping with this chartered commitment, Costa Rica has been proud to be at the forefront of advocacy efforts for the complete prohibition and elimination of nuclear weapons[2]

---

[1] United Nations, *Charter of the United Nations*, 24 October 1945. Available from www.refworld.org/docid/3ae6b3930.html (accessed 17 October 2015).

[2] Costa Rica was unilaterally disarmed and demilitarized in 1948 following its entry into the *Treaty for the Prohibition of Nuclear Weapons in Latin America and the Caribbean* of 1967 (also known as the Treaty of Tlatelolco) in which the 33 States parties pledged "to keep their territories forever free from nuclear weapons" and "to endeavor to banish from its homelands the scourge of a nuclear war". See Treaty for the Prohibition of Nuclear Weapons in Latin America and the Caribbean, Agency for the Prohibition of Nuclear Weapons in Latin America and

and for the mitigation and elimination of the disproportionate threat presented by small and medium-sized armaments to communities besieged by regional conflict.[3] For decades, Costa Rica has believed that the presence and proliferation of all weapons—from nuclear weapons to assault rifles and ammunition—violate the collective commitment that was made to disarmament in the United Nations Charter and we are committed to leading a culture of demilitarization that puts disarmament at the front and centre of international peace and security.

The United Nations Charter and general and complete disarmament

The United Nations Charter outlines clear expectations on the issue of disarmament. Chapter III, Article 11(1), states, "The General Assembly may consider the general principles of cooperation in the maintenance of international peace and security, including the principles governing *disarmament and the regulation of armaments*, [emphasis added] and may make recommendations with regard to such principles to the Members or to the Security Council or to both." Chapter V, Article 26, states, "In order to promote the establishment and maintenance of international peace and security with the least diversion for armaments of the world's human and economic resources, the Security Council shall be responsible

---

the Caribbean, S/Inf, 652 Rev.3, 29 January 2002. Available from www.opanal.org/wp-content/uploads/2015/08/Treaty_Tlatelolco.pdf (accessed 22 September 2015).

[3] The socioeconomic aspect of small- and medium-sized armament production is an important part of security problem. The production and utilization of weapons diverts scarce resources from development for less developed countries. Indeed, in a time of environmental, financial, food and energy crises, the armaments race presents an outsized socioeconomic burden to those who can least afford it. The squandering of resources on armaments that would otherwise be routed into other community projects has a domino effect on regional and community human security and development.

for formulating, with the assistance of the Military Staff Committee, plans to be submitted to the Members of the United Nations for the establishment of *a system for the regulation of armaments.*" [emphasis added]

These articles serve as the foundations, or the "jumping-off points", from which a path towards general and complete disarmament should have been navigated and eventually achieved. However, in the 70 years since the signing of the United Nations Charter, the Organization has not come close to wholly securing international peace and security, nor has it accomplished general or complete disarmament and, if current trends continue, it is not likely that such ambitious goals will be fully achieved in our lifetimes. Indeed, many would argue that the authority of the Security Council as the arbiter of peace, security and disarmament has been eroded beyond repair. This is a very common view at the United Nations.

Not so for Costa Rica. In fact, we are determined that United Nations Member States should increase, not resign from, their efforts to meet their chartered obligations on peace and security in general and disarmament in particular. Costa Rica believes that our collective inability to (yet) achieve our common disarmament goals does not mean that we should resign from the United Nations project. There remains too much at stake. We live with threats from armaments that the original authors of the United Nations Charter could barely have imagined and there are new threats on the horizon that we ourselves have not yet conceived. We believe that there is no more important treaty than the United Nations Charter, and no more important goal than general and complete disarmament.

Importantly, it must be understood that, just because disarmament is written into the United Nations Charter, disarmament can *just happen.* Instead, it is the responsibility of each successive generation to live up to and progressively work towards disarmament in the name of international peace and security. We believe that the Charter remains a living, breathing document that can—if we let it—shape the contours of our future peace. Costa Rica is committed to using the Charter—our global peace and security treaty—in discerning and navigating our collective path towards a world free from the armaments and armed forces that function as instruments of war.

Article 11 of the United Nations Charter

Article 11 of the Charter is important because it distinctly establishes disarmament as an issue of international peace and empowers the General Assembly to take action on the issue. Disarmament falls under the purview of the General Assembly's First Committee—a group that has not been lax in compliance with its duties and has maintained a high level of activity on disarmament affairs. Its accomplishments include three special sessions of the General Assembly devoted to disarmament[4] (with calls for a fourth special session on disarmament in the pipeline since 1995), the creation in 1952 of the United Nations Disarmament Commission, the creation in 1980 of the United Nations Institute for Disarmament Research, the creation in 1982 of the Department of Disarmament Affairs (known presently as the United Nations Office for Disarmament Affairs) and the adoption of numerous seminal resolutions on disarmament.[5]

---

[4] Special session of the General Assembly devoted to disarmament, convened during its tenth session (1978); special session of the General Assembly devoted to disarmament, convened during its twelfth session (1982); special session of the General Assembly devoted to disarmament, convened during its fifteenth session (1988).

[5] Among its remit of disarmament resolutions, the United Nations General Assembly has passed resolutions on ammunitions, the Arms Trade Treaty, the Biological Weapons Convention, the Chemical Weapons Convention, counter-terrorism, military spending, missiles, regional disarmament, small arms and light weapons, and the United Nations Register of Conventional Arms.

The problem with Article 11, however, is that resolutions of the General Assembly are non-binding on Member States. The preceding Article 10 specifically notes that the General Assembly may only make *recommendations* [emphasis added] to the Members of the United Nations—there is no physical means of enforcing Member States' compliance. However, this limitation may also be seen as its power. The General Assembly is the world's most diverse political space for the creation and development of global standards of behaviour and its resolutions serve as conduits for norm development—no matter how incremental these developments may appear to be at face value.

In fact, the power of the General Assembly to create so-called "soft law" can lead to the establishment of important norms in the field of disarmament. For instance, in 1991 the General Assembly established the United Nations Register of Conventional Arms (UNROCA)[6] on the premise that "being open about armaments may encourage restraint in the transfer or production of arms, and can contribute to preventive diplomacy".[7] In no way is UNROCA a comprehensive census of the global armaments—many Member States have been politically hesitant to provide full disclosure of their arms capabilities and UNROCA has faced its fair share of criticism that the voluntary information "does not include adequate quantitative or qualitative data on the weapons or contextual information on the transfers".[8] The same report, however, concludes that despite recalcitrance by Member States, "nearly

---

[6] United Nations, *General Assembly Resolution 46/36* of 6 December 1991. Available from http://www.un.org/Depts/ddar/Register/4636.html (accessed 17 October 2015).

[7] United Nations Office for Disarmament Affairs, "United Nations Register of Conventional Arms". Available from http://www.un.org/disarmament/convarms/Register/ (accessed 17 October 2015).

[8] Siemon T. Wezeman, "The Future of the United Nations: Register of Conventional Arms", *Stockholm International Peace Research Institute Policy Paper No. 4 (August 2003)*, p. 7. Available from http://books.sipri.org/files/PP/SIPRIPP04.pdf (accessed 17 October 2015).

all countries have embraced transparency in armaments as a norm and an absolute necessity, and they continue to issue statements that underline the importance of transparency".[9]

Article 26 of the United Nations Charter

Article 26 links the accumulation of arms with the maintenance of international peace and security and gives the Security Council, in tandem with the Military Staff Committee, lead responsibility for disarmament and arms reductions. The Security Council has been unable to fulfil Article 26, however, for two reasons.

Firstly, Article 26 ran into difficulty because the Military Staff Committee—imagined by the authors of the United Nations Charter "to advise and assist the Security Council on all questions relating to the regulation of armaments, and possible disarmament"[10]—was never realized. By the time the Security Council convened its first meeting in 1946, it was already beset by the difficulties inherent in having two ideological enemies—the United States of America and the Soviet Union—required to act in unison for any decision to be made. As a result, Security Council resolution 1 of 25 January 1946 was to be the first and last resolution on the organization of the Military Staff Committee. The lack of a Military Staff Committee should not in itself have been enough to derail any disarmament progress by the Security Council. But it was, historically, a contributing disabling factor that required the Security Council and the United Nations as a whole to find alternative means to fulfilling the disarmament aspiration of the Charter.

---

[9] Ibid., p. 26.

[10] Article 47 (1). Its other primary responsibilities were to advise and assist the Security Council on all questions relating to the Security Council's military requirements for the maintenance of international peace and security, the employment and command of forces placed at its disposal.

Secondly, Article 26 runs into difficulty because it does not confer upon the Council authority to take binding decisions on general questions of disarmament. In general, only resolutions adopted by the Security Council under Chapter VII, with respect to situations that it determines to constitute a threat to international peace and security in accordance with Article 39, are enforceable by mandatory measures, including economic means and the use of military force. The Council has never determined that the lack of fulfilment of Article 26—establishing "a system for the regulation of armaments"—constitutes such a threat.

Of course, the Security Council has authority to enact binding measures in specific situations that threaten international peace and security owing to the lack of any comprehensive solution to the question of disarmament. In particular, if the Security Council determines that a State's "possession of certain weapons, judged on the basis of its previous conduct, constitutes a threat at to international peace and security",[11] then the Council is fully empowered to impose disarmament obligations on that State.[12] These measures can relate to the removal of specific types of arms or to the location and disposition of armed forces.[13]

The long-held assumption that "the [Security] Council cannot impose general disarmament obligations on [all] States, for example, by prohibiting the development, production, or possession of a particular type of weaponry"[14] is coming under increasing scrutiny with the advent of thematic resolutions (as opposed to country-specific resolutions). Such thematic resolutions seek to create new global legal regimes and obligations on all States, although their scope has been quite

---

[11] Stefan Talmon, "The Security Council as World Legislature", *The American Journal of International Law*, vol. 99 (January 2005), p. 183.

[12] The most well-known examples include Security Council resolutions 687 (1991) and 707 (1991) on Iraq.

[13] Consider Security Council resolution 660 (1991).

[14] Ibid.

narrow.[15] In 2004, the Security Council unanimously adopted resolution 1540 (2004)—a thematic resolution that establishes a general obligation for all States to "refrain from providing any form of support to non-State actors that attempt to develop, acquire, manufacture, possess, transport, transfer or use nuclear, chemical or biological weapons and their means of delivery".

Even as the use of chemical weapons has become an increasing concern in recent years, no such general obligation exists with respect to conventional armaments, despite their ceaseless proliferation and daily use in the commission of heinous acts against civilians. Nor has the Council been inclined to adopt general measures to deal with nuclear disarmament, despite recognizing in 1991 that "the proliferation of all weapons of mass destruction constitutes a threat to international peace and security".[16] The promise in Article 26 for "a system for the regulation of armaments" thus falls victim to the same limitations of non-bindingness that besets the General Assembly under Article 11.

Working our way towards security and stability

Costa Rica believes that disarmament is a process, not an event. This was the point made in 2008 by Costa Rican Permanent Representative to the United Nations, Ambassador Jorge Urbina, when he said,

> The regulation or limitation of armaments should be understood as one element of the broader and more comprehensive design for the maintenance of international peace and security. It should be seen as part of the toolkit the United Nations has at its disposal to enhance the stability of international

---

[15] See also Vesselin Popovski and Trudy Fraser (eds.), *The Security Council as Global Legislator* (Routledge: 2014).

[16] Note by the President of the Security Council, document S/23500.

relations, development and peaceful settlement of disputes.[17]

As such, small but significant steps towards the reduction of armaments—such as the 2008 Summit Meeting of the Security Council convened by then-President of Costa Rica and Nobel Peace Prize Laureate Óscar Arias Sánchez—all make positive contributions towards this broader goal.

The comprehensive regulation and limitation of arms—synonymous with the objective of general and complete disarmament—is at the heart of the system for collective maintenance of international peace and security embodied in the United Nations Charter. Indeed, to the founders of the Charter, disarmament was to be a primary mechanism to facilitate achievement of the purposes and principles of the United Nations.

For decades, the General Assembly has exercised a leading role in disarmament and it should continue to do so in the future. Moving forward, it is also imperative for the Security Council to broaden its disarmament toolkit to reinvigorate proposals for general and complete disarmament. This is necessary in particular to confront contemporary threats and challenges posed by conventional weapons—not just weapons of mass destruction.[18] The maintenance of international peace and security not only requires that the Security Council be nimble and swift in its responses to security crises, but that it also be capable of taking proactive steps to deal with emerging security issues. This must also include general measures to confront threats posed by conventional arms before they materialize into breaches of international peace and security.

---

[17] Letter dated 10 November 2008 from the Permanent Representative of Costa Rica to the United Nations addressed to the President of the Security Council, document S/2008/697.

[18] Dan Plesch, "The South and Disarmament at the UN", *Third World Quarterly*, vol. 37, 2016, pp. 1203-1218.

In this regard, the Security Council should consider how the establishment of a comprehensive system for the regulation of arms—and general and complete disarmament more broadly—is not just a singular goal in and of itself, but a part of a spectrum of policies and practices that contribute to defusing tensions, building trust, strengthening collective security and bolstering regional stability. To this end, it is equally imperative that the Security Council engage new civil society voices into this effort. Civil society offers a wealth of creative and innovative ideas and there is a storied history of humanitarian disarmament campaigns succeeding where the United Nations failed—the International Campaign to Ban Landmines, the Cluster Munitions Coalition and the International Campaign to Abolish Nuclear Weapons, being prime examples.

It is not too late to recover and revive disarmament processes at the United Nations. Indeed, as advocated by the Strategic Concept for the Removal of Arms and Proliferation, it is necessary that general and complete disarmament remain a prominent ultimate objective of the United Nations system. This approach has prompted Costa Rica to be ready and willing to be a leader by example on this ambitious goal.

General and complete disarmament: The way forward

Dan Plesch
Director, Centre for International Studies and Diplomacy
School of Oriental and African Studies, University of London

Kevin Miletic
PhD candidate, Centre for International Studies and Diplomacy
School of Oriental and African Studies, University of London

It is fortunate that a clear diplomatic and technical strategy is available to contain and reverse the current and accelerating drift to increasing inter-State war and major power confrontations. Absent such a strategy, as Henry Kissinger puts it, disaster is guaranteed if we continue business as usual in negotiations and in bureaucratic practice.

This clear diplomatic and technical strategy embraces Articles 11 and 26 of the United Nations Charter and article VI of the NPT. It is founded in confidence- and security-building measures, the elimination of weapons of mass destruction (WMD) and the regulation and reduction of existing and future conventional weapons; so realizing the objective of general and complete disarmament (GCD). This strategy is available from www.scrapweapons.com. These concepts of course require political will, but it is hoped that their mere existence can begin to change the political dynamic. As looming crises are starting to drive leaders, Governments and the public opinion to search for more non-military solutions in an increasingly unstable and crisis-prone environment, these concepts will be of increasing use.

Technical soundness of general and complete disarmament

The know-how for a global system of weapons control and disarmament exists, albeit neglected. From the *United States*

Program for General and Complete Disarmament in a Peaceful World,[1] which was part of John F. Kennedy's diplomatic response to the building of the Berlin Wall, to the Arms Trade Treaty and the recent United Nations Security Council resolution 2231 (2015) on the Iranian nuclear programme, the international community has accumulated a wealth of technical knowledge and practical procedures that is now in decay and ought to be exploited to its fullest potential. Much remains to be done within the mandate of past disarmament agreements.

From small arms and light weapons to confidence- and security-building measures to WMD, every aspect of disarmament can be effectively addressed by building on tried and tested achievements in this field. Indeed, there is no need to reinvent the wheel, past agreements already provide a comprehensive set of measures that can be adjusted to cover all types of weapons in a practically achievable manner.

Elaborated in the Basic Elements[2] of an internationally legally binding agreement on general and complete disarmament developed in the Strategic Concept for the Removal of Arms and Proliferation of the School of Oriental and African Studies, University of London, with a view to revamping past best practices, there are various agreements upon which the international community can rely to pursue its objectives more efficiently and build a disarmament agenda for the twenty-first century.

---

[1] United States Department of State, *Freedom from War: United States Program for General and Complete Disarmament in a Peaceful World* (Washington, D.C., United States Government Printing Office, 1961). Available from http://dosfan.lib.uic.edu/ERC/arms/freedom_war.html (accessed 5 August 2016).

[2] School of Oriental and African Studies, University of London, "Basic Elements of an internationally legally-binding agreement on General and Complete Disarmament". Available from http://www.cisd.soas.ac.uk/Files/docs/9934634-basicelementsgcd-draft-resolution-text-jan-2014.pdf (accessed 5 August 2016).

The following technical provisions provide, in conjunction with the provisions of the Chemical Weapons Convention (CWC), proven mechanisms to carry out the verified elimination of WMD, supporting technologies and infrastructure: those developed by the South African model for dismantling nuclear weapons and production equipment; those developed for Iraq by the United Nations Special Commission established pursuant to Security Council resolution 687 (1991) and the International Atomic Energy Agency with respect to nuclear and biological weapons and their production facilities; and those developed in the Joint Plan of Action to ensure the peaceful use of Iranian nuclear energy.

The Sea-bed Treaty, the Outer Space Treaty and the five nuclear-weapon-free zone (NWFZ) treaties (Bangkok Treaty, Pelindaba Treaty, Treaty of Rarotonga, Treaty of Tlatelolco and the Treaty on a Nuclear-Weapon-Free Zone in Central Asia) offer a framework for the prohibition of the emplacement of nuclear weapons on a given territory. Parties to the NWFZ treaties may also consider bringing these in broader regimes addressing confidence- and security-building measures and conventional weapons.

The Intermediate-Range Nuclear Forces Treaty (INF) sets a precedent for the verified elimination of an entire class of missiles and launchers of such missiles, and all support structures and support equipment associated with such missiles.

The European agreements on Conventional Armed Forces in Europe (CFE) and the associated confidence- and security-building measures and open skies regime provide an institutional platform for the regulation of conventional weaponry and exchange of information on and verification of all category types within the aforementioned agreements.

The Inter-American Convention on Firearms and the Kinshasa Convention offer a framework for the control of small arms and light weapons, their ammunition and all parts and components that can be used for their manufacture, repair and assembly.

Clearly, these agreements need to be updated and adapted to specific contexts. The traditional GCD approach focusing on "WMD-conventional weapons" also needs to expand and include, without minimizing difficulties associated to them, cyberweapons, autonomous weapons and other new technologies, as well as new measures to deal with other United Nations Charter norms, including the peaceful resolution of disputes and the ban on threats or use of force. These were all included in the early GCD proposals and remain quite relevant.

Nevertheless, the disarmament toolbox is already full of proven mechanisms upon which one can draw to develop a comprehensive and quickly implementable GCD programme. Indeed, the tools at our disposal provide tried and tested practical measures to get to grips effectively with a broad range of disarmament issues. The real problem here does not lie in the alleged impracticability of or technical difficulties linked to GCD but rather in a lack of political will to put diplomatic muscles behind action points or plain and simple ignorance of what GCD means and what it has to offer.

Accommodating the bewildering antinomy of general and complete disarmament and political realities

Surely, disarmament is a politically sensitive issue. In a context where enhancing national security is understood as modernizing and building up military capabilities while testing each other's reaction capacities, the disarmament agenda has lost political ground and diplomatic traction. As a result, the link between disarmament and security and its importance as a cornerstone of international stability have been utterly ignored, except by those who assert that "security" or "peace" are necessary prerequisites for disarmament to occur. This is of course a thinly veiled rationale for indefinite possession.

However, the cost of overlooking disarmament does not serve States' interests in the long term. The conceptual fathers of the "security dilemma" have long warned us that flexing muscles may make sense from a national perspective but it is likely to result in eroding trust and furthering instability at the international level. Interestingly enough, our predecessors during the cold war were aware of this security dilemma and saw the need to counter its harmful consequences by putting in place a disarmament and arms control framework aimed to enhance both national security and international stability.

We should recall that, during the late 1980s and early 1990s, many negotiations were conduced in parallel (INF, CFE, START[3] I and II, CWC) and these were successful partly because they generated synergy. At that time, States had adopted a comprehensive approach to disarmament, very much in line with the GCD principles, where simultaneous negotiations were held in parallel on a wide range of issues such as nuclear, chemical and conventional weapons. Revisiting this comprehensive agenda in pragmatic and operational detail—not just vague aspirations—would be politically desirable especially in times of crisis as a countercyclical stimulus that contributes to defusing tensions and building trust.

GCD and this comprehensive agenda found around the end of the cold war have much in common as they share the same principle of fostering de-linked synergies and mutually reinforcing efforts in order to minimize the factual linkages between different types of weapons and create the conditions for progress. Concretely, this could take the form of a Helsinki process-bis where baskets of issues that have an impact on strategic stability are identified and discussed in parallel. Each basket would deal with a specific system of weapons, such as non-strategic nuclear weapons, high-precision conventional weapons and ballistic missile defences, among others. This process would be carried out without prejudice to progress on

---

[3] Strategic Arms Reduction Treaty.

the global disarmament programme and with a view to seeking agreement on those immediate measures that would contribute to the common security of nations and that could facilitate and form part of that global programme.

Rehabilitating general and complete disarmament into the mainstream debate

Refuting the arguments that GCD is impractical and alien to political realities is the first step in putting GCD back in the frame as these are the most deep-rooted and detrimental assertions made against GCD. But this effort of revitalizing GCD does not stop there; other steps need to be taken, such as the following:

(a) *Highlighting its advantages over the inadequacy of the step-by-step approach.* The step-by-step approach focuses on "partial measures" designed to micromanage very specific problems and disregards the broader spectrum of issues. On the contrary, the comprehensive approach put forward by GCD allows one to overcome the limitations of this compartmentalization of issues by developing a holistic and globally extensive understanding of the range of possibilities for disarmament. In other words, GCD is an attractive alternative to the shortcoming of pursuing disarmament challenges on an incoherent, piecemeal basis, based largely on improvised responses to crises du jour.

(b) *Developing synergies with existing disarmament campaigns.* GCD is not designed to replace but rather complement existing disarmament campaigns. It can serve as an umbrella under which disarmament campaigns focusing on different topics can develop synergies thereby pursuing their objectives in a mutually reinforcing manner and galvanizing all efforts towards a common goal.

(c) *Developing a policy research agenda.* This needs to include the definition of what States are entitled to retain for international reasons pursuant to the duty of the State to retain a monopoly on the use of force and holdings by private contractors; the potential for globalization of past disarmament agreements; the economic/fiscal impact of disarmament; the link between disarmament and collective security; the interface between small arms and light weapons categories and the lower sizes of weapons under the existing CFE arrangements; and lessons learned to be shared between the experience of European arms control and humanitarian disarmament processes.

(d) *Raising elite and public awareness.* As a first step, this could take the form of directing elite and public opinion towards getting the United Nations Security Council to focus on Article 26 of the United Nations Charter and follow-up on Oscar Arias' initiative in 2008 to bolster the discussion on the establishment of a global system of weapons control and disarmament.

Looking beyond general and complete disarmament: The United Nations Charter

It appears that GCD is both a practical instrument and a political necessity. On the one hand, it offers a realistic means to reconcile WMD disarmament with conventional arms control by providing concrete and practically achievable steps. And on the other hand, it offers a tool that paves the way for global military de-escalation and charts political and diplomatic ways of strengthening the Charter's system for maintaining international peace and security.

As important as it is, however, GCD is not an end in itself. It serves an even broader global good: international peace and security. Unfortunately, I fear that few understand what this term GCD actually means.[4]

---

[4] Remarks to the conference on "Promoting the Global Instruments of Non-proliferation and Disarmament: The United Nations and the Nuclear

As highlighted above by the United Nations Secretary-General, despite the deep fog of misunderstanding enveloping this concept, GCD is an essential and non-optional stop on the road to saving succeeding generations from the scourge of war. Postponing the moment when we seriously tackle GCD will only result in failing to fulfil the goals and obligations imposed by States on States as set forth in the United Nations Charter.

Acknowledgement

The intellectual basis for this article stems from "The South and Disarmament at the UN" in the *Third World Quarterly 2016*; presentation to the United Nations Conference on Disarmament on "Transparency and General Disarmament", SCRAP, 2014;[5] presentation to the United Kingdom House of Commons on a "Strategic Concept for the Regulation of Arms Possession and Proliferation", SCRAP, 2008;[6] and *The Beauty Queen's Guide to World Peace*, Politicos, 2004.

Challenge", New York, 31 May 2011. Available from http://www.un.org/press/en/2011/sgsm13608.doc.htm (accessed 5 August 2016).

[5] Available from http://www.cisd.soas.ac.uk/Files/docs/83747500-presentation-to-the-un-conference-on-disarmament-transparency-and-general-disarmament.pdf (accessed 5 August 2016).

[6] Available from http://eprints.soas.ac.uk/7658/ (accessed 5 August 2016).